If you are new to homeschooling, thinking about homeschooling, and especially if you are unhappily homeschooling - read this book. It will save you hours of time, tons of frustration, and a backpack full of money. **Deschooling Gently** *is an intelligent, practical, frank, and fearless guide on how to take the "school" out of homeschooling in order to raise children who are happily educated, life-long learners. Tammy Takahashi gently shows you how to redefine curriculum and other schoolish concerns as a set of goals and tools with limitless possibilities that will help your children be the best they can be. Buy several copies and sprinkle them around the house as constant touchstones to maintain balance, flexibility, fun, heart, and meaningful purpose in your family's homeschool life.* **Deschooling Gently** *is one of the best homeschool books I've read and destined to become a classic for homeschoolers in the 21st century!*

> *- Diane Flynn Keith*
> *Author of Carschooling, Editor of Homefires.com, Founder of UnviersalPreschool.com, and Publisher of ClickSchooling*

Deschooling Gently *highlights all the "biggies" new home educators are concerned with; socialization, curriculum, schedules and records. Tammy has a gentle way of speaking. She is good friend who is familiar with our secret fears. She shows us that all these fears are the "monster under the bed" and keeps us company while we gather the courage to chase them away.* **Deschooling Gently** *has advice for the newbie and the seasoned home educator. It is a "must" for every home schooling library.*

> *- Melissa Zawrotny*

Over my 30+ years of homeschooling advocacy, I have noticed that the biggest issue faced by parents is the need to deschool themselves — to shed the trappings of school that so often impede learning rather than support it. The idea that children are natural learners who can be trusted to interest themselves in arithmetic, reading, science and history is foreign to those of us who are products of learning institutions. But Tammy Takahashi found her way to that trust and has provided a very useful roadmap for the journey.

> *- Wendy Priesnitz*
> *Editor of Life Learning Magazine & Author of School Free and Challenging Assumptions in Education*

Deschooling Gently

Deschooling Gently

A Step by Step Guide to Fearless Homeschooling

Tammy Takahashi

Hunt Press
Los Angeles

Hunt Press
Los Angeles, CA
www.huntpress.com

ISBN 978-0-6152-0877-0

First Edition

Printed in the United States of America

2 3 4 5 6 7 8 9 10

ACKNOWLEDGMENTS

This book would not have happened without the patient help of many friends and family.

My publisher, Angela Hunt, believed in this book from the outset. She encouraged and supported me throughout the process, prodding me when I dragged my feet. Angela is the solid foundation that this book is built on.

Laureen Hudson, my editor, was my much-needed second pair of eyes. She made this manuscript shine. Without her, I would be lost.

My family put up with my hours of seclusion, my daily conversation about the process of writing, and my emotional ups and downs. My husband's support, specifically, deserves recognition. Not only did he spend a lot of time with the kids while I was writing, he also let me bounce ideas off of him and he encouraged me when I was feeling tired and scattered. My children, of course, are the basic motivation for this book. Without them, I wouldn't be homeschooling.

I also must thank my dear friend Elizabeth Scott for helping me hone my ideas. She is my ideal reader, being a relatively new homeschooler who took her son out of school in first grade. She is also a wonderful writer and a great editor.

My friend, Melissa Zawrotny, is an incredible supporting force in my life, and I owe her a big thanks.

I also want to thank Diane Flynn Keith, Michelle Barone, Martin and Carolyn Forte, Karen Taylor, Ann Zeise, Robin Saunders, Barbara Carlson, Pamela Sooroshian, and all the other homeschoolers who I have worked with over the years, who have supported me and encouraged me to write.

I'd like to give special mention to my two writing groups: Home Educator's Writing Group (http://groups.yahoo.com/group/HEWG)

and the Writer Circle (http://groups.yahoo.com/group/writercircle). The members of these groups are an inspiration to me and have challenged me to be a better writer.

All of my blog buddies deserve a high-five as well. My blog post "Deschooling Gently" was the first draft of this book. The feedback and conversation on my blog gave me valuable guidance.

Last, but of course not least, I'd like to thank the HomeSchool Association of California for choosing me to edit their bi-monthly magazine, *The California HomeSchooler*. The challenge and joys of being the *CHS* editor was an essential part of my inspiration to become an author.

All of my friends (both online and off) and my family are an important part of my life. Thank you, everyone, for being there and being supportive.

TABLE OF CONTENTS

INTRODUCTION

Discovering Deschooling

I first heard the term "deschooling" five years ago on the Homeschool Association of California (HSC) Yahoo! Group e-list. I was new to homeschooling, and I didn't think the concept of deschooling really applied to me, since my kids had never been in school. Over time, I found the deschooling discussion to be, in fact, the most valuable of them all.

Whenever someone would voice their concern about "doing things right", or when their kids were reluctant to study, I would read the discussion with rapt attention. I am a perfectionist, and I wanted to do things right. I wanted to avoid potential homeschooling pitfalls. Repeatedly, the advice these parents received was, "take time to deschool." I was curious about it. Why did the questions that I felt the most inspired to read always lead to a discussion about deschooling?

Commonly, the suggestion offered was to take one month off for every year the child was in school, and basically do nothing. This time frame was about how long experienced homeschoolers said it took them to find their educational sea-legs, and for their kids to feel good about learning again. It was often referred to as a time to detox from school.

As you might have already experienced, this suggestion wasn't always met with enthusiasm. Spending a few months letting the kids do "nothing", sounds great coming from the other side of experience. As a new homeschooler, this sounded to me like educational suicide. I wasn't alone in my fear, as other new homeschoolers would respond hesitantly to this advice, "Do "nothing" for six months? Sit around and watch TV and hope and pray that my child will spontaneously jump up and ask to do school work? How is that going to help my child to love learning again?"

It was intimidating, yet strangely exhilarating, to imagine educating my children in a way that didn't look like school. Could I do that? Was it possible? What *was* our life going to look like if it didn't reflect my own education? I wasn't confident in the idea of not having my own experience to fall back on. Even though I did want to do something different than school, the opposite extreme of no school at all left me looking at my hands wondering, "Well, if not school, what then?"

I noticed that not everyone had the need to find an alternative to the school-at-home approach. For some families, replicating their own school experience at home was an effective and enjoyable approach. Although that worked for others, my husband and I knew right away that this approach wasn't going to work for us. We decided to homeschool because we wanted freedom and opportunities. Why make the decision to teach our children differently, and then do exactly what they'd be doing in school? I wanted to create a more personalized learning experience for my children.

Yet, since I had never experienced education any other way, I was reluctant to fully embrace a life without it. I was on a journey to find a balanced way to deschool.

As I became an experienced homeschooler myself, I discovered my own answers to the many questions about how to learn as a family. I was then able to respond to new homeschoolers' questions with confidence and empathy—I identified closely with what they were going through. The more experience I had as a homeschooler, the more I would help other new families find their way, primarily by relating my own stories and describing some of the effective tools and approaches that other families used. I found myself in the position of being the one who started responding with, "take time to deschool", because it works.

I have asked myself if there was a way to learn to work together at home without deschooling. I wanted to be sure that I wasn't moving from one "this is how you do it" paradigm to another. I didn't want to follow advice blindly simply because I didn't know what else to do. Time taught me that while deschooling isn't necessary for successful homeschooling, it does come with many benefits. The main benefit of deschooling is that we go through the process of learning how to educate our children one on one within the context of our family and the world, rather than using strategies best designed for group instruction in a school setting. We learn that whatever teacher role we take on at home has to be different than what teachers at school have to do. There are different variables to consider than what school teachers have to deal with. Teaching at home is like running a small business, not running a large corporation.

I was also concerned because deschooling sometimes seemed like a way to run away from our responsibilities as homeschooling parents. The idea of letting the kids do "nothing" didn't fit in with my idea of responsible parenting. After time, and careful consideration, I saw that deschooling was in fact the opposite. "Doing nothing" is really another way to say "doing more".

Deschooling is an exploration into what's possible. Educating our children without school allows us to see that the world is a limitless expanse of opportunity. But it does take some time and experience to see past the curtains and look outside the classroom. Pattie Donahue-Krueger, in an essay called simply "Deschooling", describes it as similar to an astronaut re-entering the earth's atmosphere. It might be a bit uncomfortable, but it's worth it.

The Good School Kid

I have a Bachelor of Arts in French and one in Psychology, as well as a Master's Degree in French.

I'm not telling you this to impress you. I'm telling you this to show how thoroughly entrenched I was in the system. My kids never went to school, so they didn't have to make the adjustment to learning without walls. I'm the one who needed to deschool.

I didn't plan to be a educational rebel, let alone a deschooling advocate. I grew up a poster child for the success of the American public school system. I was the teacher's pet, earned good grades and stayed on the honor roll for most of my high school and college career. I was on the fast track to Ph.D. acquisition. I wanted to be a professor.

Then, a few weeks after obtaining my M.A. from the University of Wisconsin, Madison, a set of fortuitous circumstances forced me to make a hard choice between my family and my schooling. Although I wished at the time that I could have done both, life pulled me away from school and into motherhood. If my husband and my children hadn't pushed me to make a choice, I would probably have my Ph.D. today. Maybe I'd have two. Maybe I'd still be there. I am forever grateful for my husband's insistence that he have a satisfying job, and my children's insistence that they be born before I was done with my Ph.D.

When I was in school, I had no idea how trapped I was in someone else's idea of success and happiness. My whole value system was based on whether my professors approved of me. My grades defined how good my life was. And even as I questioned the validity of the teaching methods I was asked to perform, and I struggled against the status quo, I never once though of breaking out and finding my true self outside of school. I was eternally happy being miserable: all-nighters studying for exams, piles and piles of reading material that I was always behind on, facts and figures I impressed professors with but which never had time to sink in because I was on my way to something else—all these things made me "happy."

I was convinced that in order to be happy, I had to be "busy" and "challenged." I was convinced of this because I never knew anything else in my life.

Not until I was a mom did I figure out what I had been missing.

I had been missing me.

Deschooling Mom

I was enthusiastic about being a stay-at-home mom with my first child. I knew it was the right choice for us. But it was a choice that came with consequences. I was home alone, left on my own to figure out how to fill my completely empty schedule. I spent hours in chat rooms. I walked around Berkeley and San Francisco with my son in the Bjorn. I would go to the classes at Gymboree everyday just to have something to do. I played hours and hours of video games. I watched Oprah. I read sci-fi novels. I did "nothing".

When my son didn't do what he was supposed to (like sleep), I found comfort with being obsessed with his schedule. I scheduled meals, my son's naps, when he nursed, when we played, when we'd go for a walk. Planning his day made it feel like it when things seemed to be spiraling out of control, it would all be OK.

But my son didn't like it. Although he was only a baby, we "fought" about what the schedule should be. He was trying to teach me how to live and let go so he could grow.

As he got older, and I had another baby, and then another, I would come to learn more and more from my kids. They didn't know the latest trends in teaching kids how to sleep, eat, read, talk, walk, or recognize colors, yet they managed to do all these things. I was looking everywhere for answers when the answers were right in front of me.

It was a time of soul searching, experimenting, laughing, crying, exploring, questioning, trusting, worrying, discovering, embracing, playing and learning to let go. I re-evaluated my point of view on education and learning over a dozen times. I swung back and forth between a strict schedule as the solution to my struggles, and a laissez-faire "who cares?" attitude.

When we decided we were going to homeschool, I read many books. I devoured them. I wanted to be the perfect homeschooling mom. I found new and improved answers in each one, with even better ideas on how to educate kids than any book I'd read before. So many great ideas, I couldn't wait to try them all. My worries would be gone, because we'd finally found the right educational approach.

And while I was going through all of this, my kids went along learning in their own way. Whatever new program I found or new perspective I had, my kids just kept on being who they were, going around me (or trying to) whenever I got in their way.

I had to go through this process of exploration to learn to trust that learning can happen without school. Because I went through my own deschooling process, with the help of my children, I discovered first-hand that people are born to learn. My children have done nothing but prove this to be true. Grades, teacher assessments, or homework – none of that tells me who my kids are, even if they were in school. I know that their truth is already in them, not hiding in school lessons somewhere.

Whether my kids are in school or not, I'm a deschooled mom. My kids deschooled me. In many ways, they continue to do so. I will always be grateful to them for that.

Deschooling, and Loving School

Even as I sing the praises of freedom from school, I'm convinced that deschooling doesn't have to mean saying "goodbye" to all that is school. Even now, there are many things I still love about school; workbooks, checklists, taking tests, being with other people who are learning things, talking with teachers and professors who are enthusiastic about their subject, trivia, writing essays, and so much more.

I use these tools differently now because I no longer feel obligated to them. I enjoy using them without because attached to them.

When I was in school, and immediately after I left, I didn't see right away the co-dependant relationship I had with scholastic tools. I was obsessed with "how I was doing". My self-worth was based heavily on my outward successes. I did many meaningless tasks simply to win approval, only to move on to more meaningless tasks in order to get that approval again.

I was reluctant to let them go and see other options as "real learning". My strict idea of what it meant to be educated diminished the value I saw in other kinds of learning. I wanted to see, and I wanted to do more. But I was afraid of letting go of the old ideas of education, and embrace something that I had never tried before.

This is a common "new homeschooler" undertone in our support groups and e-lists. The questions that come up are often related to getting children to do school work or wanting to know what out-of-the box ideas we can come up with to basically trick kids into learning what they would normally learn in a textbook. That was my perspective too, until, over time, it became increasingly obvious that education is a fluid idea, defined by our own expectations. If we change our expectations and desires, the entire meaning of education changes. What a powerful way to embrace learning at home!

Getting away from "school" doesn't mean that we have to give up the educational tools that we are familiar with. In fact, learning to educate at home isn't about the tools at all. Opening ourselves up to the possibilities of how we can fulfill a child's educational needs shows us that the underlying reasons we educate, and our larger perceptions of what education is for, will have a much larger impact on our homeschooling success than whether or not we use the right tools.

Deschooling Through Wine Country

About a year ago, my husband and I went to Sonoma to take a vacation without the children. We drove up the California coast to spend a week tasting wine. We had a guidebook, which clearly spelled out how to organize a week-long vacation. All the places in the book sounded fabulous. Since there were so many wineries to choose from, we decided to follow the book's plan.

When we arrived at the La Rose hotel in Santa Rosa, we reviewed our guidebook carefully. I wanted to make sure we didn't have any holes in our wine-tasting learning. (Even after deschooling, I still found myself going back to my old habitual thinking.)

The information was overwhelming. In order to cover all the bases, we were going to have to get up at the crack of dawn, drive all day to six or seven wineries, and come home late. To get it all done, we would have to do this, not for one day, but for five.

As I looked at my itinerary, I started to become less interested in wine tasting. It just didn't seem fun anymore. All the hard work was going to quickly become tedium.

Before my husband had a chance to protest, I asked the woman at the hotel front desk where she thought we should go. She said, "The book is for tourists. Don't use that. You're going to do this right!"

I was thrilled that an "expert" was going to help us! She asked us what kind of wine we liked, and what kind of experience we were looking for—small and cozy or lots of merchandise to choose from; planned tours or free meandering. We told her our preferences, and she marked about a dozen places on the map.

The next day, map in hand, we headed out to the first winery, ready to go do this "right". When we arrived at the first winery, we started talking to the server, and she told us "Ah, those wineries you have on your map are good, but *these* are the ones you should go to." Then she circled some more wineries.

This scenario repeated itself at every winery we went to.

At first, we wanted to take everyone's advice. We were going to do this "right"! We were also very enthusiastic about how much there was available to do. After the first day, however, it was clear we couldn't take everyone's advice. And since everyone's advice was different, how could we determine the most important places to go?

The truth is, there was no best way. And there was no way we could cover everything and still enjoy the journey. When we realized this, we started listening to advice in a different way. We listened to what people told us, then we made our own decisions. After a bit of time and experience making some mistakes, we were confident that we would find our own "right" way.

On the third day, we took our time and visited only a few wineries. We didn't get to see everything. Instead, we got to know more about wine and the people behind the wine than if we had we tried to do things according to the book. There was no pressure to get it all done. We could stay and chat with the sommeliers as long as we liked. We could savor a series of Syrah and not worry about missing out on the Cabernet.

When we looked at the tour book after our trip, we saw that we had skipped most of the suggested destinations. But to be honest, it didn't feel like we missed anything at all.

Deschooling is seeing the "official" school guidebook as supplementary material, so we can circle our own destinations. A guidebook, or a curriculum, only touches the surface of the infinite possibilities. Deschooling moves us away from being married to the standard way of doing things, choosing when and how we join the crowd, and exploring the world in a different way. That doesn't necessarily mean we have to throw away the guidebook (although we can if we want to, and still be successful.) But after deschooling, when we pick up that guide book, it is easier to know which parts will be useful.

Deschooling Is the First Step Towards Success

Disengaging ourselves from school takes time. And, if there are serious family issues or we no longer have a positive relationship with learning, it will take even more time to sort out our baggage. When we move to a new country, or change jobs, it takes a while to acclimate. Deschooling is an opportunity to move toward success, one step at a time.

You might find that this process will challenge your expectations in ways you may not have experienced before. Deschooling gives you permission to release yourself from the binds of wanting learning to look a certain way. By the end of this process of exploration, I am predicting that problems and roadblocks won't be as scary. After deschooling, you'll be stronger because you will have a new way to find options for effective problem solving.

The suggestions and questions offered in the 10 steps of *Deschooling Gently* are designed to create direction during a time that might otherwise seem aimless. And although I think being aimless is a fine way to deschool, and can be an effective path for creating an educational foundation, we don't have to choose aimlessness during deschooling if we don't want to. Let's redefine "doing nothing" during deschooling to "doing nothing that hurts our relationships with each other, or our children's relationships with learning."

I hope to give you a lot to think about, and to help you come to your own conclusions on what's important for learning. In the end, you are the parent, and you have the American right to educate your children the way you prefer. I also hope that you will consider alternative viewpoints as well, particularly those that come from your children. Children don't generally have a lot of control in their lives in our society. Perhaps you can join me in changing that reality one child at a time.

A Note about Unschooling

I've been asked if I'm an unschooler, and if this book is about unschooling. My answer is "yes" and "no".

Unschooling is a movement that is often misunderstood. I grapple myself with the implications of what it means to have that label. There are many aspects to the unschooling philosophy that make sense to me, and there are others that don't. I don't like to limit myself to one school of thought on education, and I see value in many viewpoints. In this book, I tried to look at the bigger picture. While many of my observations might parallel the unschooling philosophy, it is important to me to give you as much space as possible to decide what's best for your family.

Deschooling has led many families to embrace unschooling, since the approaches can be so similar. But in the end, deschooling is what you make of it. I don't feel it's my place or my job to tell you what to think about education. Instead, it's my hope that some of the observations and suggestions in this book will give you a chance to reevaluate the meaning of learning at home, so that you may come to an independent conclusion of what works for your family. I've pulled from many different ideas of how to teach and how to learn to help you come up with a flexible process for finding your own educational philosophy.

All the methods and approaches out there can be confusing to sort through: unschooling, deschooling, classical, Waldorf, Montessori, eclectic, school-at-homers…they are endless. The beauty is that none of them are inherently better than the other. They are all wildly successful in their own right. Just ask the families who choose these paths. They will all tell you how great it works for them. Take this as a sign that each one has its merits. There is no requirement that you choose any particular method over the other, or that you choose one at all.

Where you end up is your choice. You may find that after doing research and experiencing life without school for a while, the freedom and flexibility that unschooling offers is attractive. Or, you may find it unsettling. Or maybe you will find yourself in a category that nobody's created yet, and you don't know if you're an unschooler or not. It doesn't matter so much whether you land in a style that has a label. It just matters that you are happy and satisfied when you get there.

So Where Do We Go From Here?

As you read this book, I encourage you to challenge my ideas, do outside research, and talk about the issues. It makes me happy to think that you'll disagree with me on some things, and agree with me on others.

There is one thing I hope you'll agree with me on by the end: Homeschooling is what you make it, not what someone else makes it. The ideas in this book, and any other information that you obtain during your family's educational process, is just part of the larger equation of what goes into how you find success. None of the authors or educators knows you, or has any direct vested interest in your family. Only you have that.

Use what works, and leave the rest. Find the part of yourself that might be afraid, but moves forward anyway. Everything you need to make homeschooling work is already inside you. It's my hope, that this book will help you find the fearless homeschooler that you have in you, and let it shine through.

Step 0: Create a Foundation before Deschooling

"My philosophy is that not only are you responsible for your life, but doing the best at this moment puts you in the best place for the next moment."
- Oprah Winfrey

That First Tentative Step

The first few months without the established structure for school can be intimidating. I remember when I was considering homeschooling my children -- oh, how I wanted someone to hand me a to-do list to help me on my way. Even if the instructions were not perfect, they would be at least somewhere to start. I read book after book, and talked to local homeschoolers, but none of the information I found gave me exactly what I needed.

Perhaps that was a good thing, because it forced me to become self-sufficient. Since there were no magic formulas, it was up to me, and the rest of the family, to figure out what our steps would be. The transition was life changing, and empowering.

It took us a long time to come to our homeschooling decision. Not everyone has the luxury of time like we did. Many families leave the schools rather quickly, and are thrust into homeschooling due to circumstance or an extremely negative school experience. Either way, making the decision, and then acting on it, can often be an emotional experience.

To make the transition easier, there are some practical steps that can provide a solid foundation for the process of deschooling.

- Find out the state (or country's) laws and requirements of homeschoolers
- Legally withdraw the child from the school he is currently attending (if any)
- Find at least one supportive person
- Gather a notebook, statistics, and articles

You might find there are other steps you'd like to take, such as contacting local homeschooling groups, or joining online e-lists, or even setting up a room for all of your "educational" supplies. Just don't let yourself think that you can't start homeschooling because you haven't done something. The only thing you absolutely have to do before you start is to make sure that you are homeschooling legally. Everything else can be settled later if you need to.

Understanding Local Homeschooling Laws

It is critical to understand the laws governing homeschooling where you live. In the United States, educational laws dealing with home education are defined at the state level.

In California, for example, there are no homeschooling-specific laws. Instead, we have educational laws and codes that homeschoolers use. This means that officially, there are no homeschoolers in our state. To be in compliance with truancy laws, children must either be enrolled in public school, enrolled in private school, or be tutored by a certified teacher.

Some states, such as New York and Illinois, have specific regulations for homeschoolers. Other states either have no expectations of homeschoolers whatsoever, such as Texas and Alaska, or only require that they meet the same requirements as children enrolled in private schools, such as California. Alabama doesn't have laws for homeschoolers, but the educational codes are such that the easiest way to comply is to use an umbrella school. Some states, such as Arizona, define who homeschoolers are, while others do not.

For more information on homeschooling laws, consult your state's homeschooling organization. General overviews of the state laws can be found here:

http://homeschooling.gomilpitas.com/directory/Legalities.htm

Laws are constantly evolving as our government and society becomes alternately more accepting of alternative education while pushing for more standards. The line between classroom-based education and homeschooling is becoming thinner. Charter schools and part-time schools are popping up throughout the country, making one wonder, "What exactly is homeschooling?" The answer to this question depends on a lot of variables, including the local homeschooling laws and culture.

Local and state-wide homeschooling organizations generally have the most up-to-date and accurate information on how to interpret the laws. The best way to find out if you are in compliance with the law is to do research on what the law actually says. The educational codes for your state are available online, and it is highly recommended that you read them yourself. There is also information online about how these laws have been interpreted. Sometimes, over time, even as the laws the stay the same, the interpretation of those laws change. Keeping up to date on the changes can be achieved through subscribing to state homeschooling newsletters, joining local and statewide homeschooling e-lists, and staying in touch with the informed local homeschoolers.

If you are in a situation where you think that homeschooling might potentially cause a problem, (for example a divorce or family court case) or if there is someone close to you who is a candidate for being aggressively unsupportive, it is even more important that you be in compliance with the laws and regulations in your state. In today's educational climate, a complication in cases where homeschooling shouldn't be an issue, but ends up being a point of contention, is the biggest legal risk a homeschooler faces.

There are many ways to find out about the local laws. The best, and easiest, is to seek out the statewide homeschooling group's laws and legalities pages.

http://homeschooling.gomilpitas.com/regional/Region.htm
http://homeschooling.about.com/cs/gettingstarted/a/legalusa.htm

It's important to do complete research on your laws. Find at least two or three sources for your information to assure that you haven't missed a potential inaccuracy or nuance.

Be wary of general homeschooling web sites which attempt to sum up each state's laws in a paragraph or two. They are a good place to start your research, since they allow you get a feel for the different states compared side-by-side. However, there are only overviews, which can be inaccurate or not up to date. In addition, some states have ambiguous laws, or no laws at all, and therefore many homeschooling communities have worked out a subtle (or not so subtle) understanding and a precedent of how to keep in compliance with local attendance codes which can't be explained in a short synopsis.

Also be alert to local schools, Boards of Education, and even some national support groups who claim to have a complete understanding of your local laws. They often don't have the experience of working with the details of the state's homeschooling laws. The local and state-wide homeschooling groups typically have better knowledge of how to be in compliance with your local laws, because they are living with them everyday.

There are some states where there is some disagreement about what the laws are, or how they should be interpreted. One of the common disagreements is in how much information and paperwork homeschoolers are required to file. If you find this to be the case in your state, continue to do research until you find a way to comply with the laws that you feel comfortable with.

During your research, don't hesitate to ask a lot of questions of many different people. Print out a hard copy of your laws and educational codes to have ready in case you need them. Also consider signing up for your local homeschool announcement list, to keep abreast of new and upcoming legislation, and the different ways that homeschoolers in your state interpret the laws.

Legally Withdrawing a Child from School

Each school district has their own procedures for withdrawing a child from school. Generally this consists of a letter or form that the parent sends to the school stating the date that the child will be no longer attending, and if the child is transferring to another school, the name of that school. In states where homeschooling is defined in the law, or is an acceptable option for meeting the compulsory attendance requirements, the letter may state that the child will be homeschooled. In states where homeschooling is not in the official educational vernacular, the letter will more likely state that a child will be attending another school, with the name of the new school included. You can find out more details about the best procedures for withdrawing from school from your local or statewide homeschooling support group.

Maintain as good of relationship with the school as possible when leaving. You never know when you might need to work with the school later. Playing nice with the school has helped many parents avoid truancy officers and other things that I like to call "post-enrollment issues". The school calling up to see "how the kids are doing" is not uncommon. And it's entirely possible to be faced with an uncomfortable moment like meeting the school secretary at the grocery store.

If you have a special situation with your school, such as an individualized educational plan (IEP), consult your local support group if you would like to decline special services. If your child has special needs, you can consult *Homeschooling the Child with ADD (or Other Special Needs): Your Complete Guide to Successfully Homeschooling the Child with Learning Differences* by Lenore Hayes for more detailed information on whether your are entitled to continued services, or have any other paperwork to do when withdrawing from public school.

You might also consider requesting cumulative files, although this step may not be necessary. For children 9th grade or lower, most items in the cumulative file are documents that parents already have, such as grades, immunization records and attendance. Another thing that might be in a child's cumulative files are "notes" about his behavior, how often he was in detention, when he saw the school counselor, and other paperwork that the school is required to have. These things are probably not necessary in most homeschooling situations. Although, if a child had a lot of difficulty with his school, it might be useful to know what kind of paperwork he has in his file.

When a cumulative file is requested from a school, they usually send copies, not the original documents. This means that the school is not letting go of these records, merely sharing them with the school or parent that has requested them. This might serve to help make the decision of whether requesting files is necessary.

Lastly, some schools don't consider a child officially withdrawn from their school until the new school has sent a letter to request cumulative files. This is determined on a school-by-school basis.

For teens, having the cumulative file may or may not be important for college entry. It certainly can't hurt to have it. If you are planning on homeschooling a teen, I highly recommend *The Teenage Liberation Handbook* by Grace Llewellyn, as a companion book during the deschooling process.

Create an Initial Support Crew

Our homeschooling began on a Monday. We passively declared our new status by not sending our son to what would be his first day of Kindergarten. He was 5. We didn't have a party, or a flag salute. We simply kept doing what we had always done. We ate breakfast, brushed our teeth, played in the front yard.

It was a day like any other day. My husband was at work and my neighbors were all either at work or walking their children to school before going to work. Yet, here I was, an official homeschooler. After months of telling people that we were "most likely going to homeschool" our son, and of mentally preparing myself, our first homeschooling day had arrived. And it didn't look any different than it did the day before.

My extended family wasn't against homeschooling, but they weren't sitting in the glee club section either. And my husband was still on the fence about the whole thing. This was a decision that weighed heavy on my shoulders. As we sat on the grass and my son rode his tricycle on the sidewalk, I felt the sudden rush of fear that comes when we follow through with a huge life decision. I felt totally and completely responsible.

Fortunately, I had been building my support crew. Mostly, my support came from two online Yahoo! Group e-lists, where I had forged online friendships with other homeschoolers dealing with the same concerns as I was. Long-time homeschoolers in the group also reassured me that everything I was going through was normal.

Perhaps more importantly was my good friend who I had met at the gym where I taught fitness classes. Of all my friends, she was particularly supportive. She was the kind of person who was supportive of anything I did, and trusted me. She asked me questions, but she didn't doubt me. She didn't mind when I said, "I just don't want to talk about homeschooling for a while," or when I started ranting about why my son wasn't going to go to school, even though both her sons attended public school.

My support came from other people, although they didn't know it. Grace Llewellyn, author of *The Teenage Liberation Handbook*, was one of my biggest sources of strength. Her book clued me in that alternative forms of education were possible. David Guterson, author of *Family Matters: Why Homeschooling Makes Sense* was also an early unknowing supporter of mine. He was an English teacher, whose wife taught their children at home. He was a role model for me, because I felt a kinship with him – a teacher whose main interest was learning and education, not defending a system simply because he was employed in it.

Deciding to homeschool reminded me what it was like when we brought our first child into the world. The support of my friends and family were crucial to my survival in the early months. So much so, I would often wonder how anyone managed to get along without the kind of wonderful support I had. I knew that people did it everyday, and I was in awe that they could survive without it. It was like water when I was thirsty to have people I could talk to about my struggles and fears, joys and triumphs.

I can't emphasize enough the importance of support. If you can't find that kind of support in a local friend, seek it online. Find a local support group. Get the support you need to have a soft place to land regularly. And offer support to others as well. Connecting with other homeschooling families is at the core of educating children at home. Without it, it's like living on an island with only salt water.

Dealing with Criticism

Once a year, our local homeschool information night touches on the topic of dealing with criticism. This is one topic that all home-schoolers, new and veteran, can identify with. Homeschoolers are a curiosity in today's world. Everyone wants to know how we do it, whether it's legal, if we know what we're doing, and how many hours we teach our kids. There are also many people who have serious doubts about its efficacy.

This level of scrutiny may come as a surprise to some new homeschoolers. Veteran homeschoolers can become weary of it. Nonetheless, criticism and probing questions comes as part of the homeschooling package.

Everyone asks questions about homeschooling: family, friends, strangers on the street, the grocery store clerk, the bus driver, and neighbors. And even if you are one of the lucky few who live in a homeschool-friendly community, with a fully supportive family and plenty of accepting and loving friends, the topic of homeschooling will probably come up frequently. Ironically, the worst criticisms (and the majority of the questions) generally come at the time when homeschoolers need the most support—at the beginning of the homeschooling journey.

When we're just starting out, we don't yet have concrete, confident answers to criticisms, and don't yet have the experience to back up our perspective. Even so, we are expected to answer questions like, "Can homeschooling work? How do kids do in college? How will they have friends?" In the beginning, we're still trying to figure out if homeschooling is even the right choice at all! We don't know the answer to the big questions. In fact, many of us are still asking these same questions to ourselves.

At the beginning of any journey, we make decisions based on the best information that we can find. But it isn't until we have experience and time to adjust our new lives, that we discover what the journey we are on really means to us, and whether we are traveling in the direction we want to go.

Most of the time, other people can identify with our life changes and choices. When we move to a new city, nobody badgers us about knowing where the grocery store is or how long it takes us to make new friends. When we start a new job, people understand that it takes a little while to get a feel for what it's like. But, with the choice to homeschool, rarely are we given this luxury. We're often expected to defend ourselves and know exactly how this choice is going to affect our future right from the start.

Like many choices people make in life, often times, the choice to homeschool just "feels" right. It makes sense from a philosophical or logical point of view. But without experience, it's difficult to explain this feeling to others who have no vantage point from which to empathize. So much of what individuals believe about education, or know about how to raise kids, come from a lifetime of experience. When others haven't gone through the experiences we have, we're the pioneers. Instead of understanding, we get questions.

The Best Defense Is a Good Offense

As with all difficult conversations where we are being put on the spot about our decisions or opinions, there are several ways we can deal with the situation:

- Try to understand the other person's point of view
- Sit down and have a long heart-to-heart
- Shrug our shoulders and walk away
- Ask them what they think and why
- Be honest and open

- Put up boundaries about what is OK to talk about
- Move the conversation on to another topic
- Discuss the topic with enthusiasm and joy
- Share information we have on hand about the topic

When it comes to homeschooling, all of these techniques can be effective. My personal favorite, however, is having an article, magazine or other resource on hand which I can pull out and refer to during the conversation.

If a conversation turns negative, oppressive or even hostile, having books and articles with hard facts available can give something concrete for the other person to refer to. There is nothing like showing that we've done our research to make other people feel good about our choices. It also provides a good way to segue out of a tough conversation.

I discovered this technique by accident. In the early part of our homeschooling lives, I was always reading a book, or a magazine about homeschooling, and I carried my current research around with me in my diaper bag. When the topic of education would come up in a conversation, I often shared my reading material as part of my sheer enthusiasm about what I had recently discovered.

The side effect of my eagerness to show my resources was an almost universal positive response I received because of it. The most amazing part of it was that if the conversation started turning negative, having a resource to refer to had the magic effect of either neutralizing the discussion or turning it positive. If the discussion was already positive, the other person was thrilled they had concrete information they could take home with them.

I soon found out that having these resources in my bag was a great way to feel confident and like a "real" homeschooler. I also became more and more willing to have conversations about homeschooling, because even if I didn't feel like having a deep conversation, I had my books and magazines to do the talking for me. I could share the information without having to defend myself. It was liberating to have a backup. And to this day, I still prefer to carry something about homeschooling with me. I feel naked without a magazine, card or flyer for our local information night.

I also think there's a certain peace of mind it brings to the person who is asking questions, that I'm serious about homeschooling, and not making a flippant decision. Having books and magazines on my person, gives people the impression that I know what I'm talking about. I find this to be particularly important to remember when I'm talking with family who care deeply about my children.

And in situations where I really don't want to talk about homeschooling (which is rare, I must admit), I can say, "We're doing the best we can with what we have. And oh, by the way, here's a bunch of stuff you can read about homeschooling. I'm going to go play tag with the kids."

I don't go out into the world with the intention to evangelize homeschooling any more than I intend to convert people to my passion for dark chocolate. Discussions about homeschooling happen naturally. And when they do, I'm prepared.

Having a ready set of resources also prepares us for our own moments of homeschooling 'freak-out's, as a blogging friend of mine calls them. Keeping a file or bookshelf of books can remind us of why we chose to homeschool in the first place. Those books or articles that gave us that initial spark and words of wisdom from authors whom we admire can be just what we need in times of uncertainty.

Some Ideas for Resources to Keep On Hand

Magazines

Home Education Magazine	*Life Learning Magazine*	
Aim Homeschooling	*Secular Homeschooler*	*The Link*
Old Schoolhouse Magazine	*Live Free Learn Free*	

Articles and Statistics

Benefits of Homeschooling: by Wyatt Webb, MIT alumni
http://alum.mit.edu/ne/whatmatters/200407/index.html
A collection of peer-reviewed articles and research about
homeschooling
http://geocities.com/nelstomlinson/research.bibliography.html
A study of adults who were homeschooled
http://www.illinoishouse.org/a05.htm
A list of famous contemporary homeschoolers
http://homeschooling.gomilpitas.com/weblinks/Famous.htm

Other

A copy of your state or local homeschooling group's publication

---

What About Truancy Officers?

> *"Fear grows in darkness; if you think there's a
> bogeyman around, turn on the light."*
> - Dorothy Thompson

When I use the term "fearless homeschooling", I don't intend that to mean that we can, or should, get rid of all of our fears. Fearless homeschooling means that we make decisions based on facts, evidence, and personal preferences—not because we are afraid. Fearless homeschooling means to move forward and do things despite being afraid. It means that we listen to our fears, and take them seriously, but we don't let them overcome us, or keep us from making wise decisions.

Thirty years ago and before, there was a definite risk in educating kids at home. The risks usually involved truancy officers "checking up" on homeschoolers, and even issuing arrest warrants to parents for not sending children to school.

Today, the risk factors in the United States have diminished to almost none. Being a homeschooler is no longer persecuted arbitrarily. Through the efforts of many individuals and organizations, the home education option has been established as indisputably legal in all 50 states. In the past thirty to forty years, precedents have been set, laws have been made and social perceptions have shifted. And even if there are still some negative stereotypes about homeschoolers, there is nothing illegal about educating without school.

Even so, new homeschoolers often don't know what to expect. When people are uncertain of their future, the human reaction is to protect one's self by putting up a preemptive defense. Because of this, even if there is very little reason to fear legal problems due to being a homeschooler, there can be a perceived need for what some people call "homeschooling insurance." Don't fall prey to organizations which promise to protect you from the homeschooling boogeyman. Once you know the realities of your true risk factors, you don't need this reassurance.

The best way to have a good defense against the fear of a truancy officer showing up at your door is to take three steps:

- Know your state laws confidently
- Make sure that you are homeschooling within the law in your state
- Join an organization that specifically supports homeschoolers in your state

The reality is that there is no such thing as homeschooling insurance. There are organizations that collect money into a pool to help homeschoolers. And there are groups who ask for money to help them promote the interests of homeschoolers. But there are no policies to hold for being a homeschooler. Giving money to a group does not guarantee that the group will uniformly protect homeschoolers in case of a problem.

Homeschooling-related incidents are rare in cases where there isn't a pre-existing issue such as a disgruntled spouse, or meddling neighbors. Of course, we can't be certain that nobody will ever question our legal rights to homeschool. But legally, we are doing nothing wrong, so there is no reason to buy our freedom. Supporting a group we believe is doing a good job supporting our rights as homeschoolers, on the other hand, can be a wise choice.

Even if we pay dues to an organization which supports homeschooling, money doesn't buy a release of fear. Understanding does. It's our responsibility to know our legal rights and it's our responsibility to be aware of any precedents set by other homeschooling cases in our state. We can accomplish that through researching what the various groups have done for homeschoolers in the past and through being involved with, or aware of, more than one source of homeschooling support.

I encourage you to support groups that help homeschoolers. But be wary of any group that:

- Promises to protect you from homeschooling dangers
- Makes you feel like homeschooling is basically unsafe and that you need their protection.
- Puts emphasis on saving people from danger rather than encouraging a sense of community.
- Has other political involvement. If they do, the money will be going for that too. Make sure that they are using the money in a way you agree with on all political fronts.
- Puts pressure on you to join.
- Divides the homeschooling community by saying who is a "real" homeschooler and who isn't. Or says that only certain kinds of homeschoolers should have legal freedom.
- Has any other indication that maybe they aren't what they say they are. Trust your instincts. Even if you can't put your finger on it, there might be something up.

Ready, Set, Deschool!

Now that you have the supporting structure for your deschooling adventure, you're ready to dig in and get your hands dirty. Enjoy your deschooling adventure!

Self-Discovery Questions:

- What are two URLs where you can find your state's homeschooling laws?
- Who can you ask if you have questions about homeschooling in your state? What is their contact information?
- Who is your support crew?
- Which two books will you recommend to relatives if they are interested in homeschooling? Do you have passages highlighted?
- When people ask you why you are homeschooling, what will you say?

Step 1: Redefine Curriculum

"Don't ask the barber whether you need a haircut."
- Daniel S. Breenberg

*"If you are distressed by anything external, the pain
is not due to the thing itself, but to your estimate of it;
and this you have the power to revoke at any
moment."*

- Marcus Aurelius

How Public School Curriculum and Textbooks Are Chosen

The pillar of the homeschooling image is a mom with curriculum in hand; ready to teach the young ones. Indeed, one of the first things new homeschoolers want to know is how and where to choose a curriculum. We want to know if it's interesting enough and challenging enough. We want to know if it's developmental or academic. We want to know if it will cover all the bases. Will it teach our children what they need to know?

The term "curriculum" is used to mean the collection of items we use to teach: the textbooks, workbooks and other ancillary material. It is a misconception that what makes education work, is buying a good curriculum. Education is far more than having the right books. Attitude and resourcefulness rate much higher than a quality printed curriculum.

Whatever might be the most effective tools to create a good education in schools, curriculum creation remains hinged on textbooks. These textbooks are by far the most important part of public school teaching methods, dictating when and how the material will be taught. Some school districts, such as the L.A Unified school district, go so far as having the same exact curricula for certain subjects at every school to make sure that all the kids are getting and equal quality of education.

Let's look at how schools choose their textbooks.

While every school and district will have slight differences in protocol, we're going to look at one imaginary K-6 elementary school in California as an example. We'll call it Everyman School.

Everyman School has chosen curricula for the different subjects, such Math, English and Social Studies. According to a revolving schedule, the curricula for each subject are updated every seven years. The school can choose textbooks from a catalog provided by the district.

After a few of the teachers try out the new textbooks on their students for a year, they evaluate the textbook. After that year, the teachers recommend the books they liked best, and the school adopts them.

For this school, they are in a district that chose the English program for them. So they have to use the same English program that all the schools in that district are using, to make sure that every child in the district is learning the same thing at the same time.

For the other subjects, the district gets a list of state-approved textbooks that match the state's educational criteria. This sounds like an effective, highly monitored process for textbook selection.

But little does anyone realize how little rigor goes into choosing the state textbooks. In fact the selection process for state approved textbooks is about as good as closing one's eyes and picking at random.

William J. Bennetta, editor and president of the *Textbook Letter*, responds to an article by Richard P. Feynman, where he describes his experience while on the committee for choosing math textbooks for California elementary schools in 1964:

> *"Recall Feynman's observation that "usually the only people to look at the books were schoolteachers or administrators in education." That is still true. In a typical case, a state agency*

creates an evaluation committee that consists of schoolteachers and school-district officials, perhaps augmented by an ordinary citizen or two. Then the agency charges this committee with the task of appraising some number of books in a given subject, even though the committee lacks anyone who possesses expert knowledge of the subject in question. The members of the committee then engage in a silly, scripted ritual, producing collective judgments about books that few (if any) members have actually tried to read—and they eventually contrive some unexplained, unsupported, collective recommendations, declaring that the books should be accepted for use in schools. They don't write individual reports, so the taxpayers cannot know who did what—i.e., the taxpayers cannot determine who (if anyone) inspected and endorsed any particular book. No one is responsible for anything.

If a state agency really wanted to obtain legitimate evaluations of textbooks, the agency could achieve this by using a process that is very well known: Send each book to a knowledgeable reviewer who will appraise it, who will write a report to set forth and explain his appraisal, and who will sign his name to his report. This is the process employed by the book-review editors of newspapers, magazines and professional journals throughout the land. It works, and it can be repeated to any desired extent: To obtain several appraisals of a given book, simply send the book to several reviewers.

As a rule, however, state agencies don't want legitimate evaluations of the textbooks that publishers submit for adoption, because the agencies are allied with the publishers. The adoption proceedings staged by these agencies are not designed to help school districts, to protect students, or to serve the interests of taxpayers. Rather, they are designed to serve the interests of the publishers, to generate approvals and certifications for the publishers' books, and to help the publishers sell those books to local schools."
    - The Textbook Letter
    July-August 1999

Our society puts so much emphasis on the importance of curriculum in schools, yet very few people know how those textbooks reached the hands of school children. Textbooks are the corner stone of a public school education, yet the way they are chosen is sub-optimal. The worst part of this story is not that these books are riddled with imperfections, but that the teachers have no choice but to use them. Fortunately, we aren't in school, so we can move away from being tied to textbooks or prescriptive curriculum.

Looking at Curriculum in a Different Way

By homeschooling, we have the opportunity to redefine what it means to put together a curriculum. Instead of using textbooks as the central focus of learning, we can make anything the central focus: games, literature, physical activity, arts and crafts, communication, the internet, or traveling, for example. If we don't want a central focus at all, we can do that. We can make our homeschooling world any way we want to, and let textbooks and other kinds of curriculum exist as our supplementary materials. The best part is that we can do this while also having a purpose.

It is our job as homeschoolers to figure out what our curriculum is. How are we going to learn? What kinds of materials will work? Where do we want to go? How are we going to set up our days?

This freedom to create our own curriculum can be intimidating. I can see why pre-packaged curriculum is very inviting when we are looking for something to guide us into the homeschooling world. I encourage you not to purchase a pre-packaged curriculum right away, however. I can almost guarantee that it will provide low returns on your investment.

Homeschooling curriculum has become a billion dollar industry. Complete curricula are available from dozens of companies. Homeschoolers obviously buy a lot of materials, or there wouldn't be so many options to choose from.

But I ask, if there are so many options to choose from, and so many curricula companies who successfully sell their wares to homeschoolers, how can any of them be that much better than any others?

The idea that homeschooling curriculum is so necessary comes from two major sources. First, the pressure to buy materials comes from the companies who sell the curriculum. These companies drive the idea that homeschoolers need a pre-packaged curriculum. They take advantage of homeschoolers who are overwhelmed with the idea of doing it all themselves. And homeschoolers buy into it, which encourages curriculum companies to sell even more.

The second reason that curriculum seems so necessary is because we are socially indoctrinated in the idea that we have to have one. Simply put, schools equate year-long pre-constructed curriculum with "education". As a result, that legacy gets dragged into the homeschooling world like a ball-and-chain.

The truth is, we don't need a fancy curriculum. We've been convinced that we do because of convention, school-oriented society and a lot of businesses trying to get our money. I admit that at first glance, this is somewhat of a cynical viewpoint. But if school didn't exist, and homeschool businesses didn't exist, and finally, the convention of having curriculum as a homeschool option didn't exist – we would all do just fine without them. The homeschoolers who existed before the information boom didn't use it. And many homeschoolers today don't use pre-made curriculum. Overall, they do just as well as homeschoolers who do use one.

All that said, I don't recommend tossing the idea of workbooks and homeschooling materials completely out the window. Instead of rejecting the idea of curriculum all together, we can redefine curriculum. Instead of being "homework and assignments that kids get in order to learn what they are supposed to", curriculum can be "a collection of tools, materials and experiences that help our children grow at their unique pace, with their unique goals and abilities in mind."

Instead of limiting ourselves to the idea that curriculum is mainly paper, computers, and output-driven materials, we can expand our definition of curriculum to include things that have no concrete product, such as communication, playing, volunteering, exploring, and observing, which encourage our children's unique abilities to shine. The supplies we get at the curriculum fairs, the pre-packed projects and all the workbooks that glint and glimmer at the bookstore are supplementary materials to the kind of real-life learning that really matters.

The school definition of curriculum is far too limiting for what homeschoolers can do. In that regard, the materials we can get from the homeschool catalogs are great tools, but in our new definition of curriculum, those things in the catalog are only a small fraction of what our child's complete curriculum looks like. With our new perspective that all these things in the catalogs are supplementary, not essential, we are no longer limited by what we can buy or put grades on. We can make better choices, and be free from that small box that the school definition of curriculum puts us in.

It's all in How We Use It

> *"Each man is unique. Nature abhors sameness. Each flower in the field is different, each blade of grass. Have you ever seen two roses alike, even of the same variety? No two faces are exactly alike, even in identical twins. Our fingerprints are so singularly ours that we can be positively identified by them. But man is a strange creature. Diversity frightens him. Instead of accepting the challenge, the joy, the wonder of variation, he usually is frightened of it. He either moves away from or endeavors to twist uniqueness into sameness. Only then does he feel secure."*
> *- Leo Buscaglia*
> *Love*

Most of us are familiar with the public school way to use curriculum. They take a pre-established to-do list, with materials explicitly designed to teach the items on the to-do list, and then move in a straight line from point A to point B. There is a clear starting point, and a clear path ahead. At the beginning of the year, you can take a school curriculum, flip forward through the pages and look to see what the students will be doing some time later in the year. There are no surprises. There are no changes. There is some room for customization, but only if it supplements the established curriculum – teachers are not able to change the direction of the curriculum itself.

If a student gets lost along the way, he's fallen behind. If he wants to go a different direction, he doesn't have a voice to change his learning path. There is little room for individual student needs. There is no freedom to say, "Wait a minute, this isn't working, let's do it a different way." There's always room to *add on* to a pre-set curriculum, but the opportunities to change direction or change the approach are harder to find.

If we look at the homeschooling stereotypes in the media, they depict mom sitting down at the beginning of the year, making her lesson plans and setting out the goals. Essentially, mom takes over the job of the schoolteacher, the school board and the principal, in deciding what is going to happen during the year. With curriculum in hand, going back and forth between the table of contents, the assignments and the tests, mom is supposed to figure out how fast to go when, how much to do in a week or a day, and which assignments will work the best and which won't.

This is a comforting vision, because it looks like "teaching". It's also comforting to want to do this, because once our curriculum is laid out, we can breathe a sigh of relief that it's all taken care of. Unfortunately, using the familiar process of A to Z curriculum construction emulates a large group education process for a small number of children. It's not real teaching, or real learning. It's busy work for mom. More importantly, it sets up expectations that are unfair for our children, because they are given the impression that they have "freedom" in homeschooling, when in reality, instead of being trapped by the school teacher's expectations of what education is, they are trapped by mom and dad's vision of education instead. Homeschooling is supposed to set us free, not move us from one trap to another.

If we compare it to a business, this scenario is much like a president of a small company creating a business plan that is modeled after Disney. Seems like a good idea because Disney is an incredibly successful business. But since they are a large company, they require a lot of large, concrete goals that everyone works together on, or there is chaos. In a small company with one, two, or even a dozen employees, flexibility, ingenuity and the ability to focus on what that company does best, instead of focusing on process, is the road to success.

To me, homeschooling is similar to the home-business model. While home businesses thrive from having a direction, and a purpose, what really gives an entrepreneurship its wings is the ability to be flexible and quickly adjust to the needs of its customers. Homeschooling parents have this flexibility. We are able to adjust it to meet our individual child's needs, moving faster or slower than anticipated or in another direction entirely. In short, homeschoolers can take chances. It's this freedom to take risks that gives homeschoolers power. Without the willingness to try new things, homeschoolers are missing a huge benefit of not being in school.

In order to have flexibility in home learning, we need a curriculum that isn't hard-set in stone. We need a set of learning tools that have limitless possibilities. We need a set of goals that give us freedom to use whatever means available to give our children opportunities to be the best they can be.

Just like a small business can't succeed if it expects its clients to cater to the business' needs, small-scale curriculum won't work if the most important thing is the curriculum's demands. Small businesses cater, within their capability and purpose, to the needs of the client. Homeschooling parents can do the same with their children. Starting with the child's needs, and working a curriculum around that, we can still use curriculum materials, and benefit from all there is out there, but in a more appropriate way. Instead of focusing on making the curriculum work, we can put the emphasis on life, family, relationships, and our goals.

Old Curriculum Ideas Keep Us Trapped

At the risk of sounding alarmist, I'll tell you that the biggest hazard of buying pre-set curriculum is becoming its slave. The minute we buy a curriculum, and have it in the house, it can so easily become the measure by which we conduct our homeschooling lives.

Pre-packaged curriculum gives us the good feeling of having everything we need in our hands. It looks familiar. It is created by a company that we assume is populated by people who know a lot more about learning and teaching than we do. But all of these assumptions are ephemeral. The only real measure of whether it will work or not reveals itself the moment we hand it over to our children. The book can feel good, it can be familiar to us, and it can be designed by experts, but all of that doesn't matter if our children don't like it.

Schools are populated with educators who are supposed to know more about teaching and learning than we do. And yet, so many kids aren't learning there. School doesn't always work, even though everything we needed is supposed to be there. School promises us that our kids will be taught well and given everything they need to be successful. We know that's not true for every child, yet it's so alluring. Even when things are clearly not working, so many parents opt to continue to search for that gem they were promised. All the while, the child is wasting time being lost.

Curriculum can be a similar kind of siren, offering so much of what we need and want, tempting us to dig in until we can't turn back. The siren's call is strong, and makes us want to continue to push through to find a solution because we've gone too far to turn back now.

Jan was a mom who came to our homeschool information night with her six year old son, Landon, who was learning to read. She had come to the meeting to get some advice on how to pick a curriculum that would work. She had tried everything, from *Hooked on Phonics* to *Teach Your Child to Read in 100 Easy Lessons*. She made organized daily plans with each, and was determined that each one would be better than the last. It would be a better progression, more interesting or less repetitious. Yet, even after all of her planning, and using the best programs she could find, her son continued to resist reading.

I bumped into the family at the bookstore a few days later, and had a chance to chat with them for a while. While Jan and I talked, the dad read book after book with the son, who couldn't get enough.

I asked Jan, "What does Landon want to do? What does he like?" She looked dumfounded. She said, "Well, pretty much anything I want to do, he doesn't." I asked if he liked games or comic books. She said, "Well, ya, he really likes those things."

"Why can't you use those things to teach him to read?"

"Well, how will I know if he's learning if I use games?" she responded.

I talked to her child for a while, and came to the realization that he was an incredibly smart kid. He could see right through his mom's efforts and knew that the programs she bought for him wouldn't be any fun. And he saw that she wanted him to learn something during those times. And he didn't want to.

So the mom had a choice, try to figure out a way to make her kid bend to the curriculums she had picked out, or to play it his way, and to make a curriculum around what he liked to do. Since she was a homeschooler, and not enrolled in any school, she had full flexibility. And the only thing keeping her from making the choice to use something different and out of the box was her own slavery to curriculum.

We can live and learn without curriculum. We have a plethora of choices in front of us to learn, including curriculum. We have the power to choose what's best for us, instead of expecting someone else, out there, who doesn't know our child, decide what is important for them to know. To can turn to our child to figure out what will work and what won't.

Pre-packaged curricula can be a powerful tool. But we can't be afraid to put it down if it's not working. If we buy into the idea that curriculum has to be used a specific way, or our children are failing, then curriculum has control over us. It doesn't have to be that way. We can see that homeschooling curriculum is bigger than that.

My friend Sarah was one of those moms who needed to take a complete break from curriculum because it was controlling her life, and making her, and her child, miserable.

She had started homeschooling with gusto. She bought *A-beka* for math and a whole K-12 curriculum for all the other subjects. She wanted to start the year out right with her five-year-old son, who was old enough to be just starting Kindergarten. Sarah set out to be super-mom homeschooler. In everything she did, she was successful and organized. This wasn't going to be any different.

Then something unexpected happened. After a few weeks of happily going along with the schedule of the curriculum she bought, her son started to rebel. He threw tantrums, begged to go to school (where all the other kids were having "fun") and wouldn't even touch the books that he loved so much when they first started.

The newness had worn off, and what was a novelty in the beginning, turned into a grueling unpleasantness that didn't match his exploratory nature.

Sarah tried everything she could to adjust the curriculum to match her son, but he wouldn't acquiesce. Finally, she got him to do his work by bribing him, and threatening to take away his privileges.

This got him to do his work. But he wasn't happy. They fought a lot. She cried a lot. And the dad was ready to put his son in school because he could see how much it was hurting their relationship.

She and I talked about other ways to educate, and how she was becoming trapped in the school mindset that she was trying to avoid by homeschooling. Then one day, she said to me, "I'm done with these school books. They are taking my son away." And she sold them on eBay. She decided to go cold turkey, and focus on doing fun things with her son.

It was hard in the beginning for her. She felt groundless. It took her some time to come up with a set of tools on her own. Instead of looking for the perfect Kindergarten curriculum, she started choosing tools in response to her son's needs. After a few months of using hands-on activities like art and playing in the mud, and doing more "kid stuff" like reading, playing ball, talking, and going to the park, her son said to her in the bookstore, "Mommy, can I get this book?" It was a math workbook with a big "K" on the front. "I'm in Kindergarten, right?"

She was so excited; she not only bought him the math workbook, but many other workbooks in the store. She set up her schedule again, sure that this was the sign he was ready to get serious about learning.

But the math book was all he wanted to do. He didn't want to work more on the workbooks. And he wanted to go through the whole book in one sitting. When Sarah saw how he devoured the math book in one moment, and then fought her about the writing workbook, she realized that she had fallen into the same trap again. So, she put all the books she bought on the shelf where he could reach them if he wanted. And while he would pull out the books once in a while, they were no longer the central focus of her curriculum. The workbooks were the supplement to a rich life-based curriculum based on games, hands-on activities, and classes at the park and rec.

Sarah took a pretty big leap putting everything away at once. There is another way, however, if you are like me and really like workbooks and being organized. There's a way to find a middle ground, where we can let go of the all-in-one $500 curriculum, yet stay within the edges of our comfort zone; I call it a piecemeal curriculum.

Creating a Piecemeal Curriculum

There are several benefits to using a piecemeal curriculum instead of an all-in-one set:

- A piecemeal curriculum is cheaper than a pre-fab curriculum
- It's easier to buy
- We can look at each element carefully before buying
- We can use each element in any way we like
- We can move on to the next level for each subject, or stay in the same level for long periods
- We can work at several levels at the same time, even in the same subject
- It can be tailor-made for each child.

A piecemeal curriculum is less stressful than a boxed curriculum, because we are not bound by a massive, expensive set of materials staring at us, and making us feel guilty that we aren't keeping up. A piecemeal curriculum doesn't claim to solve all of our homeschooling needs, nor does it "feel" like it has to be followed in a certain way, within a certain amount of time. When we buy piecemeal, we remove ourselves from the rails of what we "should" be covering, to the freedom of what we "could" be covering.

The piecemeal curriculum is designed slowly, one element at a time. You can get bits and pieces anywhere you can find it. And anything counts as part of the curriculum. It could be books, raw materials, or experiences. The pieces can be found anywhere: bookstores, museums, garage sales, online, teacher stores, your friend's library (please, ask first), Grandma's attic, used-book sales, the library, the park, the local art store, the backyard, homeschooling conferences, craft fairs, or the zoo. You create a piecemeal curriculum by using material you find in *your* world. Everything you ever need is available in the places you go and through the travels of your life.

As you can see, we can find materials and books anywhere. But the piecemeal curriculum is not just about where we find our treasures. The *way* we pick books for our kids is perhaps even more important.

Instead of looking at books and activities as a way to fill a child's mind with the "right" kind of things, and to make them smarter, try selecting the pieces of your curriculum from the framework of, "will my child thrive from using this?" Don't think like a teacher. Think like a parent or a friend. Put yourself into your child's perspective. You know better than anyone else what would put a smile on his face. Choose materials that you can both feel good about.

Some questions to ask ourselves when we are buy curriculum pieces

- Will my child like the topic?
- Will he like the presentation?
- Will he like the activities?
- How about the feel of the book?
- Does it have enough hands-on activities?

- Does the content look like it would be fun?
- Can I imagine my child grabbing a hold of this and smiling?
- Does this material appeal to my child's way of seeing the world?

Different Children Need Different Kinds of Pieces

Having three kids, I find myself creating a different kind of piecemeal curriculum for each of them.

Generally speaking, nine-year-old son likes puzzles, games, codes, how-tos and intricate explanations. He likes to take what he reads in a book and immediately put it to use. He likes word puzzles, jigsaw puzzles, and any activity where he is required to use his hands or his body. He prefers books that have activities he can do right now, with little prep. He also likes to build things. So, for his piecemeal curriculum, we get him things like Mad Libs, crossword puzzles, code breakers, back-yard science experiment books, building materials, and workbooks that have these kinds of activities in them.

Our seven-year-old daughter has another take on life and learning. She prefers books with a lot of pictures and visuals, books that allow her to tell a story, activities that she can take her time to finish, color by numbers, puzzles that end up with a picture as the result, and workbooks that don't have a lot of clutter on the page. When we buy materials for her, we get her books with vivid pictures like comics, paints and markers, freeform drawing pads and workbooks that have lots of short activities that allow her plenty of time to practice her favorite skills before moving on to something new.

Our four-year-old is a little easier, since she's happy at this point to play with almost anything the bigger kids have. When we do buy something for her, it usually appeals to her love of all things pretend and all things tiny.

Kids are constantly changing, however. And what they like now may not be what they like tomorrow. So we buy a variety of items, and watch. Think of this as an educational experiment, and not a mandate, after purchasing new materials.

The beauty of the piecemeal and "experimental" process is apparent when we hit on "that" first book that our child steals from our hands, takes to his room, and we don't see him again until dinner. When we hit the jackpot, everyone feels good. They learn. We learn. And we learn that "yes!" we can indeed figure out how to teach our children without spending an uncomfortable amount of time, money, and angst on a program that we were sure was going to work.

There will be times when the kids won't like the pieces we pick. This is, actually, a good thing to have happen. As parents, we learn from when our kids say they don't want anything to do with the material we've offered them. We haven't made a huge investment in it (hopefully), so instead of feeling that we have to force the child to do the work because it cost so much money, we can let it go, and find another book or activity that they might have a better relationship with. Also, it is entirely possible that our child isn't ready now, but will be soon.

The Kids Don't Know They Are Learning

Another great side effect from this kind of curriculum approach is that the kids won't be hyper-conscious that they are supposed to be learning something. If it's a book or activity they enjoy, they think they are playing a game, not learning. They are having fun with no boundaries and not being made to do schoolwork. We, as parents, know they are learning. But since it's challenging in a way that interests them, kids won't learn to fear it when we say it's time to do schoolwork, or if we say we're learning a lot from an activity. They won't be thinking in those terms. They will be learning, instead of thinking about learning.

Have We Really Let Go of School When We Buy a Workbook?

In addition to being attached to our teaching materials because of their monetary value, it is also possible to have an emotional attachment to the idea that if we have something, we are wasting it if we don't use it. I know I've felt that way before about things I have bought for both myself and for my children. It's a legitimate human feeling.

The first step to avoiding this kind of emotional attachment is to recognize if we are apt to feel this way. If we are, we can make note when we buy something to ask ourselves, "Will I be OK if my child doesn't like this book? Am I going to be OK if it sits on the shelf for a few months before he finds it interesting?"

With any book or activity, there is a chance a child just won't be interested. Or perhaps, he won't be ready. If we go into the purchase accepting this possibility, we will be able to make better decisions about whether it's worth the money. It will also force us to carefully consider whether the book is good for *our child*, or if we're buying the book because *we* like it.

There is nothing that has to be done right now. If we don't buy a math book right away, or we go through a few chapter books before we find one our child likes, there won't be any tangible consequences. Learning is not about production and proof; it's an internal sense of accomplishment. Learning can't be rushed. But it can only be inspired to take off on its own.

If we buy a book to add to our piecemeal curriculum, allowing our children to have whatever reaction to it that they like gives them room to create their own relationship with the material. Approaching curriculum in this way also allows us to see each piece as part of the deschooling experiment, learning who our children are, their likes and dislikes, and their overall learning habits and preferences. Having all these bits and pieces of different kinds of curriculum materials around gives us parents a window into a child's world.

Games: The Secret Homeschool Weapon

In 2002, we went to our first homeschooling conference. I really wanted to homeschool, but didn't have my foothold yet on how I wanted to go about it. That all changed when I heard the first speaker. Her name was Carolyn Forte. And her talk was about something called a "Games Curriculum."

That perked up my ears! A curriculum based on games? That's exactly what it was.

In an article called "Game Plan for Learning" in *The Link*, Carolyn writes:

> *"Games and activities can greatly enhance your homeschool experience. They can give you a break from the ho-hum of a packaged curriculum or they can be your curriculum. Either way, they are a great way to learn. One reason they are so effective, is that there is less pressure to perform with a game. Children don't usually feel threatened by an age appropriate game and a feeling of safety is the most important component in being ready to learn. Children often develop learning blocks in subject areas that have threatened them. Put the same things in a fun game format, and you will be amazed what happens. This is assuming that the child is developmentally ready for that concept. If you get resistance, even in a game, put that game on the shelf for a while longer. Your child may not be ready. Now go out and have some fun!"*

When she said that games could be our curriculum, I just about fell out of my chair. She was so right, and I had never thought of it! Even if we do nothing else, ever, the kids can learn just about anything from games.

She described how games come in a box and they can be made on the fly. Any activity can be made into a game, even cleaning the house or doing laundry. Set a timer, and see who can clean their room the fastest, or who can pick up the most Legos. When driving, we can play a game to count how many blue cars we see, or see if we can stump each other with trivia.

Carolyn also passed out a handout with a list of games for each grade and each topic. (Available from Excellence in Education at http://www.excellenceineducation.com) When I saw the list of games and how they could be used for education, I knew right then that we could homeschool our kids.

We had already been playing games, even before the kids were born. And now, a few years later, and the kids are older, games have become a learning staple in our home. (In fact, as I write this, my son is trying to get me away from the computer so we can play Doodle Dice.)

Games Resources

- *Carschooling* by Diane Flynn Keith has many games for learning in the car
- *Games for Math*, *Games for Writing* and *Games for Learning* by Peggy Kaye are collections of pencil and paper games for elementary school. (Although some of those games were a challenge for me too!)
- *Hoyle's Rules of Games* by Albert H. Morehead, Geoffrey Mott-Smith and, Philip D. Morehead explains the rules for more than 250 games including Rummy, Solitaire, Scrabble and Chess.
- Knucklebones (www.kbones.com) is a magazine for the board game enthusiast.
- FunandBoardGames (www.funandboardgames.com) is a game review website.

Out-of-the-Box Curriculum

Anything and everything has curriculum potential. As you explore more of the many possibilities, think out-of-the-box about what to put in your teaching toolbox.

Consider including books that teach the same kinds of material that workbooks present, but in different ways. Think self-study books like *Teach Yourself Calculus* by Hugh Neill, which are intended specifically for learning outside of a classroom. Books like *Lies My Teacher Told Me* by James W. Loewen and *Grossology* by Sylvia Branzei and Jack Keely are also good alternative choices to traditional school books, because they draw us in to look at history and science in unconventional ways. The *Klutz* kits are interesting too, for even though they are often hands-on projects, they also go into the history and culture of the craft, as well as how-to explanations.

Lauri's Story: *"When I first looked into homeschooling, I was convinced that I would need to buy a box curricula for my children because I am not creative enough to come up with my own curricula. I was fortunate to attend the Homeschool Association of California Conference that year and heard the remarkable Paula Harper Christensen speak on child-led learning. It was the message I needed to hear which freed me to explore the many approaches to homeschooling.*

I had a lot of fun learning about packaged curricula like Calvert, the Waldorf approach, Five-In-A-Row, Charlotte Mason, The Well-Trained Mind, and the list goes on and on. I have become an eclectic homeschooler who likes to choose a bit here and a bit there from the many options we have available. I like learning history chronologically as opposed to the way most schools teach and both Charlotte Mason and The Well-Trained Mind advocate this approach. When I began homeschooling, I liked using the Five-In-A-Row approach; I can use my wonderful local library, read books to my children and help them learn geography, language arts, science, history and art. I also enjoy using the unit study approach to help my children learn things and then we sometimes add the lapbook method to help them document what they've learned.

Right now we are in a co-op learning about the US Presidents. Each child draws a president's name from a hat and puts together a report on their president. My youngest son loves learning about each president and really enjoys finding out all the interesting details of his life. I love that we can do an activity like this that he *so clearly enjoys. My other son really gets into the lapbooking part of this exercise. He gathers all the information he needs and then puts his creative efforts into a theme for his lapbook. For Abraham Lincoln, he made the Abraham Lincoln Memorial Pamphlet and the cost of the pamphlet was $5.03. The $5 bill has Lincoln's image as well as the penny, so the price fit the subject. He found lots of interesting items to include in his report, including the various movies in which Abraham Lincoln was portrayed and by whom. It's been a fun co-op and we are nearing the end. I think the next subject we will explore is "inventors".*

It is especially fun finding educational games. Here are a few we enjoy: Stratego, Professor Noggin card games, Quick Flip, Set, Rummy Roots, Mille Bornes, Geoshapes, Apples to Apples, Constructionary, Visual Brainstorms, Chess...the list could go on and on.

Isn't it great that we have so many paths we can choose from to make our homeschooling journey a success?"

Welcoming Want-To's

Unfortunately, I can tell you from experience that even piecemeal curriculums can be a money sink. They can be a time sink as well. Most of the best ways to learn don't cost a dime. The free learning experiences are the vast majority of what makes up our life. Taking a walk, talking with our friends and loved ones, reading, thinking, and pursuing our hobbies are essential to every homeschooler's curriculum toolbox. Workbooks and other school-oriented books are a supplement to the real life experiences that makes us who we are. This is deschooling, there are no educational shoulds or have-to's. Right now, it's time to focus on want-to's. The majority of have-to's can come later.

To the human brain, meaningful work is the most satisfying and stimulates the most growth. Children are willing to do difficult tasks and work hard when they are doing what they love to do. We can create this by using our children's want-to's as the foundation for building an effective learning environment. In other words, we can come to understand our children's learning currency, which is the underlying motivation for everything they do.

It's human nature that the more we work on projects that have meaning for us, the more enthusiasm we have for life. Our brains look for opportunities to feel good. When we feel good about something, we want more of it. Doing meaningful work feels good. When we like what we are doing and it has value for us in some way, we are inspired to work hard to make it happen.

Another way to look at it is from an efficiency perspective. Children have a different perspective on time than we do. An hour to us flies by in a flash. To a child, it can be an eternity, especially when they are very young and bored, or frustrated. Efficiency gives time new meaning for a child: if the time he spends working on schoolwork is interesting, useful, fun and at his level, then he won't even notice the time passing. Anything you put in front of him that doesn't match all of these criteria slows down his reality. And when a child is spinning his wheels in slow motion, there is very little learning happening, except learning that learning is boring.

Sheri's Story: *This is our deschooling story.*

1) I made the decision to just do it. This was by far the hardest step and it took years to finally reach it. I think I had been waiting for some magical sign from the Heavens to give me the courage, but as I'm learning, courage comes with the act and not before it.

2) One morning, I picked up the phone and called my daughter's school and told them that she would not be returning.

3) I wrote a letter to my local School Board notifying them of my intent to homeschool and copied the school principal. The only reason I was required to do this was because she had already been enrolled in school. My province's guidelines do not require notification to the School Board if the child has never been registered. I also am required to submit a new notice of intent every fall.

4) I cried. Seriously. Once it was done, it was like a dam had burst. Relief and fear overwhelmed me when I realized that I had actually done it. Now that I had, I began to wonder if I even could do it. Could I be a good teacher? Was I really helping my child or was I hurting her? Real concerns that I had to face head on.

5) I joined two local on-line homeschooling networks and went to an information session night at the library.

6) I turned my house upside down looking for anything that would serve as learning material—everything from reference books on animals and plants to craft supplies and flash cards. In the 6 months since we started homeschooling my biggest expense has been our field trips. (You don't have to spend a lot of money to help your child learn…thank God, because I don't have a lot of money.)

7) I created a ridiculously rigid schedule that I felt, at the time, would make the transition to homeschooling easier for both of us.

8) I burned the schedule. Who was I kidding? The idea that there would be an easy way through this in itself was silly, but to think that making our lives more like school was going to help at all…well, that was just delusional.

9) I accepted that I didn't have all the answers, that I will never know the future and that the only way through this was just to do the best that I can.

10) I started blogging and discovered a wealth of information, resources and kindred spirits.

I don't cry anymore. I am a good teacher and I have been helping my daughter. I wouldn't know that if I had never tried.
- Reprinted with permission from
http://www.matteroffaith.com

What If My Child Misses Something?

Here's the truth about living life: every day, every moment, we are making choices. And with every choice we make, there is always at least one choice, if not many, that we didn't make. That means that at every moment, we are missing out on something.

Yes, our children will be missing out. No matter which choices we make, we miss out. That is the reality of living life, and making choices.

Homeschoolers get to do a lot of things that school kids miss out on. We have picnics at the park for lunch, go on a day trip on a whim, go on road trips off season, visit with friends for hours, and do volunteer work that others can't because they are in school. In addition, the kids don't get exposed to as many illnesses (like lice). And when they do get sick, they can take as long as they need to get better (and don't get behind in work). They have time to read as many books as they like, they aren't rushed through their activities, they can be who they are, and they aren't pressured into dressing a certain way or being beautiful… the list goes on and on.

Yes, homeschool kids DO miss out on things. And I sometimes get sad that my kids won't experience some of the really good things I experienced in school. They are leading a different life than I knew as a child. But they are happy. They have full and interesting lives. So, even if they are missing out, they aren't at a disadvantage. It's like this – people who grow up in a small town are missing out on big city things. People, who grow up in a big city, miss out on small town things. Neither is inherently better. But both are "missing out." When all these people get to be adults, they can recover some of the things they thought they missed. But whichever path they take, they are going be OK.

People all over the world are living experiences that are different than our own. There are people who live in a completely different socio-economic class, people who don't do much except work and sleep, and people who spend every single day woodworking or playing soccer or watching TV, for example. Yet, these people are happy. There are tons of happy, joyous people who are living simple, focused lives, and who are missing out on the million other things that exist in the world.

Are their lives less meaningful because they missed out? Only if we judge the value of their lives by what they didn't do, rather than judging their lives by the happiness they experience from the things that they *are* doing.

The feeling like we are missing out only exists inside our own head. It doesn't come from actually missing out on something; it comes from our own emptiness somewhere in us. When we feel we are missing something, it comes from fear that we aren't good enough just as we are, that we are somehow less than perfect because we don't have something that others have. This fear grips us, and we become jealous or envious, desiring to be a part of the larger group and do what everyone else is doing.

The way to assuage this fear is to look at who our children are now, and ask – are they whole? If they are, they are not missing out. If they aren't whole, then it's time to identify which needs aren't being met, and to meet them. Rarely is there only one way to meet a need. If our needs are met, we don't miss what we don't have.

With a piecemeal curriculum, we have the freedom to identify and meet the needs of our children. We don't have to wait to see what comes in the box, or ask permission to move ahead or veer off the track. We can go whichever direction we want to. Instead of seeing it as missing out on something that would have come in the box, we can see it as embracing the life we are creating for ourselves.

Self-Discovery Questions:

- Which topics interest your child?
- What kinds of books does he tend to check out from the library?
- How much are you willing to pay for a workbook?
- Are you willing to put a book down if it's not working and move on?
- Where in your community can you find books on the cheap? Where in your community can you find a variety of workbooks and self-learning manuals?
- What kinds of books, besides textbooks and workbooks, would interest your child?
- What elements besides books are important in a curriculum? Keep these in mind while exploring the next chapter: "Exploring Options in the Real World."

Step 2: Exploring Options in the Real World

"You have to leave the city of your comfort and go into the wilderness of your intuition. What you'll discover will be wonderful. What you'll discover is yourself."
       - Alan Alda

"We live in a wonderful world that is full of beauty, charm and adventure. There is no end to the adventures we can have if only we seek them with our eyes open."
       - Jawaharal Nehru

Life and learning is bigger than curriculum. The tools we use to learn and teach are stepping-stones to get to the big purpose: to live in the world and thrive.

The best way to prepare for living in the real world is to go out and be in it. Not only will we find things to discover, to explore, and to learn; out in the real world, we find ourselves.

Self-Discovery Instead of Education

Deschooling reminds me of what it's like to end a relationship. When we finish a relationship with someone, especially someone that was entangled in our emotions, the vision of who we are and what our life was about revolved around doing things together with that person. We have too many memories just to "forget" the person, shrug one's shoulders, and move on. It takes a while to remember who we were before we were with them and to redefine what our new life is going to look like alone.

When we start homeschooling, we are leaving our old ways of practicing education. When we no longer have the familiar dance of teacher-parent-child, we instinctually want to replace the missing dance partner.

We can have a rebound relationship with another educational model, or we can re-learn who we are after ending our toe-to-toe relationship with school. It's a time to make our own decisions without sitting around waiting for the phone to ring.

Relationship gurus and counselors suggest several things when dealing with a break up.

- Throw away everything that reminds you of that person. Everything. Having them in the house, and in your vision, makes the transition even harder.
- Avoid places that you used to go to together.
- Join a club, start a hobby, and otherwise find new things to do.
- Spend time with friends and family who will support you in your new life.

A loose translation of this advice is, instead of sitting around wondering how it's all going to work out now that we are missing a part of what used to be our everyday life, get out of the house and do new things. Get started right now with moving on.

In deschooling, it's no different. Get away from trying to teach. Make a break from pushing the kids to learn. Instead of wondering how they are going to learn to read, go to a story time. Instead of worrying that they won't get into college, go to a science museum. Instead of looking in a book to find the answers to how to get your child enthusiastic about history, go to a re-enactment or see a movie.

Or, if you spend a lot of time worrying about education in general, go to the beach.

Gain some space and perspective. Get out and discover who you and your children are. Help them discover themselves by recreating their view of how they fit into the world.

When we start to get wrapped up in our own heads about the right thing to do, how to live our lives, how to teach, how to learn, if we're doing it right or if we are making the right choice, we're missing opportunities. We can get so busy thinking about how we might be missing out; we're actually making ourselves miss out!

Finding ways to get out into the real world is the key to ending the interior monologue. It's also an effective way to finding homeschooling balance.

Distraction Isn't Just for Preschoolers

Dr. Sears, and many other classic parenting gurus, advise parents to deal with screaming toddlers or preschoolers with distraction. Instead of running head to head with our little ones, bring up a whole different topic that will get their attention, and help them forget about what they were so upset about before.

If you've used this technique, you've probably noticed that it's a great way to get connected with our kids while helping them deal with stress.

This technique works well for preschoolers who have a short attention span. It also works well for us homeschoolers.

If you start to feel that antsy feeling like you're supposed to be "doing something to teach the kids something important", an internal parental panic attack might be coming on. If these thoughts of worry start making your heart pound in your chest, or you find yourself snapping at people randomly, it's time for a "get out of the house" break. Distracting ourselves by focusing on a project or field trip is a great way to deal with deschooling panic attacks.

Go to the mall, to a friend's, for a walk, to the beach, swimming in the lake, to a farmer's market, or on a nature hike. Do things you love. Do the things your kids love to do. Just get out of the house, leave your school books behind, and go adventuring in the real world.

Real World Spur of the Moment Adventure Ideas

Museums
Amusement parks
Movies
The beach or a pool
Chuck E. Cheese
Arboretum
Taking a walk around the neighborhood
Calling up a friend to get together
Going to the park
Kicking around or tossing a ball
Ice skating
Rollerblading
Biking
Farmer's market
Watch the sunset or sunrise
Go fishing
Going for a drive to the mountains, desert, hot springs, or other
natural landmarks
Go bowling
Visit a farm
The zoo
The pet store
Kite flying
Walk a mall
Bookstore
Library
Pet adoption center
Get your nails done or a facial
Race remote control cars or helicopters
Video game arcade
Draw with chalk on the sidewalk
Open lemonade stand in the front yard
Work in the garden

Having Fun vs. Learning

When we go out to do new things, should we choose things that are fun, or things that are meaningful and educational? Most of the activities listed in the above chart are fun and playful activities.

Having fun is an important part of life that often gets overlooked. When our to-do lists are full, and we're feeling the weight of shoulds, there is no better time than to go out and enjoy ourselves with the people we love. Having fun with our children creates happy memories together, one of the building blocks of a strong relationship. Doing enjoyable activities on a regular basis creates enthusiasm for life, and a tapestry of positive experience, which we can look back on again and again.

But is there such a thing as having too much fun? Having fun can be addictive when used as escapist activities. If we go out and have fun when we are feeling stressed about homeschooling, isn't that a way to run away?

There are two kinds of fun: fun that is hedonistic, and fun that is meaningful (or purposeful).

Fun that is purely done for the sake of feeling good in the moment is absolutely necessary. It frees us from having to always be "on", allows us to let go and relax, and gives us a chance to appreciate the moments we are in simply because they are good right now. Not every moment we are experiencing something new does it have to be educational. There is huge value in sitting deep in the moment, and experiencing the ride.

Meaningful fun is different. It's fun that we have, and at the same time, we grow. We are learning something about ourselves, about the world, expanding our imagination, tweaking our perspective or building relationships. Meaningful fun is enjoyable to experience, while at the same time it has lasting positive benefit.

One of the first hurdles in deschooling ourselves, and our children, was remembering that life is good. Getting out into the world to have fun is meaningful in the beginning of our deschooling journey because it is the first step in creating a positive feeling that life is enjoyable.

After a while, however, having fun purely for having fun can get old. We might also worry that we're having too much fun and not doing enough to encourage growth and increase understanding of the world. If we go to the beach everyday, we might start craving other kinds of activities besides building sand castles or body boarding.

That is a common worry, and it's worth thinking about.

It's OK to spend a lot of time doing fun activities, even if they don't seem educational. But it's also OK to bring in more activities that do double duty by being enjoyable and purposeful.

The True Path to Happiness and Successful Deschooling

According to Tal Ben-Shahar, a professor at Harvard, and author of *Happier: Learn the Secrets to Daily Joy and Lasting Fulfillment*, activities and choices which truly make us, as humans, happy, fall into both categories: fun and meaningful.

Ben-Shahar describes four kinds of approaches to activities and life:

- Rat race
- Hedonism
- Nihilism
- Happiness

The rat race, as Ben-Shahar describes it, is what we are taught in school. It's also the most widely accepted perspective towards success in our American culture. We are taught early on that we have to suffer now, and get through whatever it takes, even if it means boring or frustrating activity, in order to secure our success in the future. The rat race is putting a high importance to meaningful or purposeful activity, with a low value on whether or not it is any fun.

An example he gives is the successful businessman. He works hard in school, gets good grades and does all the after school activities he thinks will get him into a good college. He works hard, and everyone praises him for his diligence and self-discipline. He has some fun, but most of his life is not about fun, it's about making sure that he is doing well in school, because that's the way to make sure he'll be successful later. Then he goes to college, and repeats the same routine, working hard and doing what he's supposed to, taking classes he doesn't like and doing homework, so that he can get into a good business school. He does such a good job, that he makes it through his MBA program. All through this he is praised for all his hard work and willingness to do what it takes to get ahead.

When he graduates, and becomes an employee, he's sure that he can finally relax and enjoy life. But he can't. Once he's got a "good" job, he has to continue to work hard, sacrifice and push to get ahead. He becomes regional manager, then vice-president, then president, then CEO. At each step, he keeps waiting for happiness to come, but it never does.

His life has been full of meaning and sacrifice, but it was lacking fun. He was successful in his work, but he was too busy working hard to enjoy it.

Hedonism is the opposite of the rat race. This is the teen who is always goofing off, never worried about the consequences of her actions, and living for the moment. When she becomes an adult, she drifts from one thing to the next, doing whatever fun thing seems interesting. This is the person everyone wants to hang out with: she has no worries and fills everyday with things that are enjoyable but have no meaning.

As she gets older, she finds that she isn't happy either. All the time doing fun things seems wasted. Who is she? What is her purpose in life? A life of hedonism seems interesting, but it's not a path to happiness.

Nihilism is when we've become so disenchanted by our past of either being in the rat race or spending all of our time on hedonistic activities that nothing seems worth it anymore. Why bother doing anything fun or meaningful, because happiness is just a ruse?

The last category is happiness. Happiness is when we choose life activities and goals that are both enjoyable and meaningful. A real "happy" moment is when we like what we are doing right now, and we consider it to add value to our lives, or the lives of others, in the long term.

Although it's fine to be a little hedonistic from time to time, to spend a little time running around in the rat race, or to even wallow for a few moments there and there in our nihilistic drudgery, a truly happy homeschooling life is when every one of us in our family spends the majority of our time being truly happy, doing enjoyable and meaningful activities.

The Benefits of Physical Exercise

One of the best activities for encouraging learning is physical exercise. Moving our bodies increases blood flow to the brain, it increases endorphins (the feel-good hormone that makes us motivated), and it gets out nervous energy.

Pat, a mom of two high energy pre-teen girls, turned me on to the idea of using physical exercise as way to decrease stress, and increase learning receptiveness. She said that every time her kids started to fight with each other, or with her, she would gather everyone up, and go for a walk or kick a soccer ball around. It was the solution that worked the best, especially in the beginning when the girls were used to losing their chance to go outside in school if they didn't finish their work. Instead of restricting access to going outside as a punishment for not doing what they were supposed to be doing, she used physical exercise as a way to redirect her girls' attention and foster a better attitude towards learning.

Physical fitness is a huge commercial industry. Our culture is obsessed with how many calories we burn or whether we're losing weight. That's a superficial benefit to exercise. Getting out and moving our bodies on a regular basis gives us much larger benefits, such as self-esteem, enthusiasm for other activities, and a healthier body overall. All of these things help us learn better.

In March of 2007, Newsweek published an article called "Can Exercise Make You Smarter." This articles reports that more and more schools are reducing P.E and recess in order to squeeze in more time for seatwork. In the long run, however, studies show that lack of exercise during the school day reduces overall learning, even if children study more.

On study they cited came from the University of Illinois. Charles Hillman gave 259 third and fifth grade students fitness tests, and then compared their grades. Overall, the kids with the fittest bodies were also the ones who had the best grades.

Physical exercise releases chemicals that actually increase brain function by encouraging brain cell growth. Some scientists call this the "exercise effect." Kids, in particular, seem to benefit over the long term from exercise. And when it comes to learning new things, physical activity increases kids' ability to learn new things, and retain what they learn.

It doesn't matter what kind of activity we choose. Being physically healthy isn't just about how long we work out or how many calories we burn. We can go outside and just have fun together using our bodies, and the benefits on all of our learning and our moods will be obvious.

Nourish the Soul First

Children are like flowers. They are born beautiful. As they grow, they slowly evolve into a more complicated, whole person. We parents can't make them more beautiful than they already are. We can only provide the space in which they can show their natural beauty.

We can provide the nourishment and encouragement, but we can't force them to grow faster. We can get in their way and make it harder for them to grow, but just like we can't make them grow taller, we can't make them learn faster just because we are impatient to see their beauty that we know is in them.

The way to give our children the most opportunity to allow their natural beauty to come through is to nourish their soul first.

Exploring the world with our children nourishes their soul like putting a flower out into the sun. Too much sun, and it burns. Not enough and it withers.

The time we spend in the world is like an experiment to see what nourishes our children. There is no right or wrong of how often or how long we should be out. We can keep our kids busy, while recognizing their need for downtime. Time to relax is just as important as time to explore. The companion activity to getting out is staying in and resting.

Have you ever watched a really good movie, and thought about it for days afterwards? Our minds are soaking in as much as we can. It's later, hours, even days or weeks after the movie is over that we can take all that input and make sense of it.

When our lives are busy with fun and meaningful activity, it's amazing what ideas will come while washing the dishes, driving, sitting outside with the kids – basically doing mundane tasks that require little or no new thinking.

Kids need this too. They need time for all the stuff that they learn to sink in, without distraction or pressure. To just mull over whatever it is that they have learned recently.

And if you have a dreamer on your hands – you know, those kids who just like to sit on the hammock outside and swing their legs – then you may find yourself having a lot more downtime than you might think is necessary.

Nourishing our children's souls is creating a balance of activity and reflection, as they need it. Just like a flower, our kids need water and sun, but they also need time to be alone in their heads.

Kids Are Adults in Training

During the time of deschooling, you might have some workbooks, you might have some other school stuff, but your number one main focus for teaching your children is taking them out into the world to give them practice for being an adult. As much as we are told it's the case, school is not preparation for the real world. School is a child's world. Preparing for the real world is knowing how to get along in the adult world. The best way to do that, is to practice being in that world on a regular basis.

Kids are not adults, obviously, and shouldn't be expected to act as adults, or to have the same responsibilities. Nor are they going to be kids forever. They are slowly learning and growing for the specific purpose of being able to one day leave the nest and function in society on their own, owning their own adult responsibilities.

Although many people leave school at age 18 fresh from the teen social pool and thrive in the adult world, it's not natural transition. Moving from being in school all day and having the responsibility to live up to other people's expectations on a constant basis into the world where nobody asks anymore whether homework is done or not takes a huge shift in perspective. It's a shift that a lot of people struggle with. Even good students (or perhaps especially these students) have a tough transition into a world where our deeds and actions are no longer translated into grades or assessment.

Allowing our homeschooled children to experience the adult world with us, surrounded by other adults who have already made the adjustment into responsible independence is the best way to teach them how to get along in the adult world. They may not be ready today to fly off on their own, but when it's time for them to do so, they will have had so much experience doing normal adult activities, there will likely be little or no transition into the phase of adult living.

One of my favorite topics to read about is the grown homeschoolers. Grace Llewllyn published a book called *Real Lives* which showcases interviews with twelve unschoolers as teens, and then again as adults. Over all, they are normal young adults, looking for meaning and purpose, like most of us are at that age. What struck me about these teens, and I see this among the homeschooled teens I've met in person as well, was their confidence and ability to adapt. None of them worked dead-end jobs; none of them were running the rat race, and all of them, once they had a dream, made no hesitation to go after it.

Homeschooled teens become normal adults who are already comfortable living in the adult world, and understand how it works.

Ideas for "Adults in Training"

- Setting up a PO Box
- Ordering a holiday meal at a catering service
- Preparing all the details for a party, meeting or formal event
- Selling and marketing a product
- Scheduling a trip including booking plane tickets and hotels, and being able to navigate getting to the destination
- Negotiating a contract
- Using a map to find a new location
- Finding the best deal on a computer or TV
- Writing a letter to the editor
- Having an interview with a potential employer or a journalist
- Conducting an interview as an employer or a journalist
- Helping the homeless or a charity
- Starting and running a club
- Making friends and business contacts
- Changing a tire or oil on a car
- Helping a neighbor with lawn maintenance
- Helping with the family budget
- Dealing with rude and aggressive people in public
- Dealing with rude and aggressive neighbors
- Talking to people about their careers and how they got to where they are
- Preparing and mailing out holiday and birthday cards
- Returning a gift to the store

- Boil an egg and make coffee
- What other skills do you think are important for adults to know?

I don't know about you, but there are many things on this list that I was never taught how to do. When I became an adult, I felt like I was expected to know how to do them, and so I was embarrassed to ask for help when I needed it. Shouldn't I know how to boil an egg? Shouldn't I know how to repair a tire? No way was I going to ask someone to show me. Too many times I've heard an incredulous, "You don't know how to do that?" Even though most of us have holes in our real-life adult-world knowledge, we still expect others to have it. We expect teens to have it to, yet where do they learn it when they are in school most of the time?

When children grow up with lots of exposure to these kinds of real world problems, they learn by watching us solve them. And then, at some point, they will help us accomplish the tasks. Eventually, they will take over the process on their own. That's the natural way to learn these things.

I must emphasize that kids in school can and do learn these things. But they have less time to learn them all. Homeschoolers have the time. We have the freedom to give our kids a lot of opportunity to practice the skills they need to have to function as adults.

Travel Schooling

Some homeschooling families have chosen to make traveling and getting out into the real world the basis of their educational method. Traveling is a high-interest, attention demanding activity that also gives lots of time for being together quietly.

Traveling is also a great way to learn the things that most kids only get to read about in books – think of all the monuments, natural phenomena, historical buildings, cultural activities and more that give an unparalleled life-long memory. Travel is a great way to go if you have the time, money and just want to get away from school.

Every year at our two statewide conferences, there is a session offered called "Adventure Schooling." David and Ann Severi tell us the tales of their recent year's worth of travels all over the world. Here is their bio from the California Homeschool Network Expo in 2007:

> *[David and Ann Severi] and their three children have taken homeschooling adventures in 42 states and 4 countries so far. They traveled the U.S. for 365 days in an RV, and they lived for a summer in Taiwan. David and Ann call their homeschooling style "Adventure Schooling." It could also be called "Away-From-Home-Schooling." They do everything they can to get out of the house and into as many environments and cultures as possible. That has meant physical environments from the Hudson Bay to the Florida Everglades (and even an Asian rainforest). It has included trips to the opera and to plays on Broadway; and it has also meant preparing and eating meals with homeless families, and helping homeschoolers in the inner-city. It has meant portraying in public the roles of a Renaissance family, a Dickensian family, a Civil War family, and a Native American family. Their passion is to encourage other families to immerse themselves in homeschooling adventures!*

Talk about a real-world education! These kids are learning not only how to get along in the adult world of their community, but about how to get along in the entire world everywhere.

The value of travel is far greater than anything we can learn in a book. My experiences abroad are indescribable compared to what I knew of Europe from books and stories before I lived there. We've driven up and down California, to Nevada, through Utah and into Colorado together. The kids have seen first hand the variety in landscapes, and people, through our local travels.

Traveling teaches us not only about places, but about people. The more we learn about how connected we all are as humans in our world, and how we are also influenced by the culture that immediately surrounds us, the more we realize that we have the power to make our lives the way we want it. In other words, traveling teaches children about themselves, and how they will one day fit into the adult world.

Of course, not everyone has the luxury to travel their entire year in an RV. Fortunately, we can still benefit from traveling by exploring our own stomping grounds. There are many ways to explore local history, math, science, culture, agriculture, the environment, politics, nature, or any other things within a weekend-wide radius. Our local areas are rich with opportunity – opportunities that most kids miss out on because they are in school. We get to go to the library when it's not busy, to volunteer at a local nursing home during the long daytime hours that seniors don't get many visitors, or take part in a play or musical that needs a lot of time that most kids can't give up.

Your local homeschooling community might have options too. Some local groups have field trips that can only be accessed in a large group, or give heavy discounts to large groups. Local groups also sometimes offer parent-led classes for free or inexpensive. Not to mention park days, play dates, and other programs. Our state-wide organizations have week-long camp-outs and conventions as well.

The World Is Waiting for Us

Life is a process, not a means to an end. The only moment we have is now. There is no such thing as getting ready to have a good life. We have a choice to make our life good right now, or not. Being a student of the world is one way to make it good. Experiencing real life activities together is part of what makes a full life.

Going into the world to live is not running away from the responsibility of teaching. It's embracing everything that exists as important parts of the world we live in. Experiences we have bring deeper meaning when we experience them first hand. We learn to get along in our world better when we are in the situations and need to use the skills without being hyper aware of those skills.

Home is a wonderful place to be. We can claim the world as our home as well. It's about finding balance and where we belong. When we have found that balance, and when we have arrived in the place where we belong, we'll know. We'll have found true happiness.

Self-Discovery Questions

- What opportunities are available in your area?
- What kinds of things have you always wanted to do but didn't have time for?
- Is there someone you know who is active in your community, from whom you can get more information on things to do?
- Try a web search for your area and look for classes, workshops, conventions, store events, or community events

Step 3: A New Kind of Schedule

"There is only the moment. The now. Only what you are experiencing this second is real. This does not mean, live for the moment. It means you live the moment. A very different thing. There's value in the past. After all, it brought you where you are. There's value in the future, but it lies in the dream, for who can predict tomorrow? Only the moment has true value, for it's here."
- Leo Buscaglia
Love – 1972

I ♥ Schedules

There were so many things I loved about school. And one of them was making my schedule. Every semester, I opened my crisp class list and I put together fifteen different possible schedules. I loved the puzzle of managing my time with constraints. I enjoyed this process more than most of the work I did in the classes themselves.

I also loved having a schedule. Over the course of the 25 years I was in school, I came to live in tune with the clock. I knew exactly how much time I had in class, how much time I had between classes and how long it took to walk everywhere. I was a compulsive early-arriver in order not to be late and mess up my schedule.

I also loved collecting class syllabi. Knowing exactly what was coming each week gave me comfort.

As much as I loved my schedules, I have to admit, they controlled me. I was compulsively early in fear of not being on schedule. I obsessed over due dates, how I never had enough time to get everything done and what I could do to work the system. I was co-dependent with my calendar. I enjoyed planning, but when I was living all the things I put on my calendar, it became a rat race.

While I was in grad school, I not only took classes, but I taught classes and I held a nearly full time job. I kept adding things to my schedule because I never felt like I was doing enough. I didn't want to miss anything. I wanted to get my degree done on time, and I wanted to get experience teaching, and I wanted to get promoted to manager at my job.

I had all the goals and enthusiasm on the track to success. But, I was so focused on where I wanted to go, I rarely was able to truly enjoy where I was. My schedule was an enabler for me to continue focusing on the future, instead of enjoying my life.

No Longer Trapped by Syllabi

True to form, the day I received my M.A. in French from the University of Wisconsin, Madison, I turned my sights on my Ph.D. Even though I wasn't even sure that's what I wanted to do, I didn't have anything else that I really wanted to do either.

I was two weeks into what I did not realize was my last semester in grad school. I had signed up for a full load, while still engaged in my teaching position, my nearly full-time job, and an extra class on the side, as per my normal over-scheduled self. Then, out of the blue, my husband got offered a job in California. It was one of those jobs that we couldn't pass up. Our move would be paid for, they'd help us find a place to live, and my husband would be paid about triple what he was earning at the time.

My husband left to set up in California while I stayed in Madison to finish up my semester.

Once I knew I wasn't going to get my Ph.D., my whole attitude towards school changed. That was the best semester in school I had ever experienced. I pared down my schedule to three things: the class I was teaching, one fun class in a subject I had always wanted to learn, and my nearly full-time job that I loved. Everything else, I cancelled.

That moment of canceling my classes was so poignant, so empowering and so liberating, I still, to this day, dream about the experience—a constant reminder of the day that I set myself free from my co-dependent relationship with schedules.

New and Improved Relationship with Time

Time is fixed. Schedules can help us manage our time. But that was only part of it. We have to make choices on how to fill that time. We can't ask for more, but we can opt to use the time with more effective and enjoyable events. Often times, we make schedules as an attempt to expand time. The more we are attached to our schedule, the easier it is to fill our time with shoulds, leaving no room for activities that are at once joyful and meaningful. Knowing that we have a choice on how to fill our time, and exercising that choice, can change our lives.

The last semester in grad school changed my life. I had put away the schedule filled with shoulds, and filled my time with want-to's. I had gone my whole life creating a schedule full of what I thought I was supposed to. And now, I had changed my life by simply filling my schedule with different kinds of things. Even though my days were just as full and just as busy, it was a better life.

Yet somehow, every so often, I felt like I was cheating. I also periodically got the rush of panic that I was messing up my life. Those times of panic resemble the feeling I have from time to time about our life at home, without school. How can I be doing a good job homeschooling if I'm not working "hard"? Believe it or not, I feel guilty about being happy, and about my kids being happy. There's still that deep down feeling that in order to be learning the "right" way, we need to be spending a lot more time in the rat race, going through self-imposed hardship in order to prepare for the future.

The Reality of Lesson Plans and Schedules

Itineraries. Schedules. Lesson Plans. When we create an externally structured life for our kids, their time is dictated by what's supposed to happen when. They don't have to think about what comes at 1 PM. They know. They don't have to figure out how to fill their time, it's right there in the schedule. It provides a lot of comfort for kids and for parents – to plan an entire semester or year or even week ahead of time. It's human nature to want to know what's coming next.

Just like curriculum, it's also easy to become addicted to it. And to feel like if we don't have a full, hyper-structured plan, knowing exactly where we are going and when, that we're lost.

The reality is this: schedules make us less afraid because it gives us a way to look away from ourselves, and to run away from the reality that we don't know how to fill our time. Having a strict, detailed structure gives definition to ourselves, and our world, when we don't know what our world is supposed to be. It gives us something to hold on to when we don't know where we belong in the world.

The less we know about ourselves or our children, and the more we use external measures of success, the more likely we are to make strict schedules and lesson plans to organize our lives.

Lesson plans are a trap, not because they aren't a good tool, but because they make it too easy for us not to think about what's important, and to let something else do the thinking for us. The trick is this—to be able to use a schedule and lesson plan in a smart, purposeful way. And to know when it's doing the thinking for us. It's scary to do things on our own, but a lesson plan won't save us from our fears. It only delays them until we eventually have to face them head on.

> **Aynsley's Story:** *"This is my first year homeschooling. I have an 11-year-old in public school and a 9-year-old and 4-year-old at home. I am not naturally organized. I thought "Oh no. I need structure for this to work." I designed plans and perfected the home classroom environment for my ADHD daughter. I bought an adjustable height table, 16" chairs, ball chair, full spectrum lighting, music with 60 beats a minute to improve self-regulation, visual and auditory timers, fights for busy hands, aromatherapy oils, schedules with graphics,*

etc... She likes structure so, I bought structured programs like Saxon math.

Big waste of money. Fast forward to real life—our structure is now that we do some of the same things every day. So many pages of reading, so many pages in this or that workbook, fieldtrips and projects that interest her for as long as they interest her. She created a lovely Powerpoint presentation on Narwhal last week. She is in a couple of book clubs and a theater class. She likes math, but Saxon is so dry we both dislike it. As soon as I cover long division we are switching to Life of Fred (funny stuff).

What I've learnt from this:
If I am bored, the kids know it.
If they are bored, I'll know it (and pay for it).
A flexible schedule is more interesting and practical.
Structure can be reading 30 minutes a day.
It does not matter what they choose to read, where they choose to read it, or what time during the day they choose to do it. It still gives me something consistent to write in my records and a provides a sense of accomplishment."

The Challenge to Make a Better Schedule

Even if you aren't convinced at this point that schedules and lesson plans can be a way to escape our true selves, I'd like to give you a challenge – take some time to let go of lesson plans and schedules. You're in a great time to try it out. Give your family a chance to discover your life rhythms and to see what happens when everyone has a chance to live without constraints for a while.

Did you just feel a mini heart attack? I felt that way too in the beginning. I know how hard it is to let go of schedules – I'm going to promise you that you can have a schedule, and you can have rhythm, with some solid sense of the future and of what's happening when. But wait a little bit. Let's take a vacation from the world telling us what we should be doing for a little while.

A balanced homeschooling life – the life you might be searching for in this whole deschooling thing – calls for a healthy marriage between being scheduled and being free. We want our children to be free to find their authentic self, and have fun during childhood, but we also see an importance of having some kind of predictability in life. Some people can live without having any kind of predictability in their lives (and most likely, those people won't need this book anyway!), but you and me, we're not in that group of people. We need some kind of base to stand on. The point of our mini-vacation from schedules isn't to turn to a life of hedonism like Tal Ben-Shahar describes. Getting away from our need to "do what we're supposed to do" and create a new rhythm based on our experience spending time with ourselves and our children, not based on what we are afraid we might miss if we don't.

Our Role as Homeschooling Parents and Teachers

As homeschooling parents, taking on the role as the teacher, we see our children looking at us for guidance. How we handle that expectation will change everything in our homeschooling life.

What you consider to be the roles and responsibilities of a parent will be unique to you. There is no ultimate right answer on how to handle our children expecting us to help them with their growth.

There are four main ways that parents teach their children, independent of the parent's homeschooling philosophy or approach:

Modeling. How we, as parents, act and respond to the world teaches children far more than anything we say.

Trust and acceptance. The amount we trust and accept our children directly affects their attitudes towards themselves and their capacity to learn.

Relationships. The more we value our relationships with our children, the more they will respect our opinions and perspectives.

<u>Listening and watching</u>. When we are able to step out of our children's learning space and take time to listen to them and watch their choices, the more we understand them and can provide opportunities for them to learn.

These elements of homeschool parenting are the most important. Making a schedule or task lists, such as lesson plans, is not what will make or break homeschooling success. Being connected to our children, knowing our life rhythms and being connected to the world is far more important.

Making Lists and What to Do With Them

> *"An outline is a crutch; there when you need it, and a solace when, in the dead of night, you think you'll never be able to figure out how to finish this project. The outline tells you it can be done, that, if all else fails, there's a working plan you can fall back on. But when you find yourself revving ahead of it, when you see things unfolding naturally, organically, spontaneously, before you, forget about the itinerary."*
> - Robert Masello
> *Robert's Rules of Writing —*
> *101 Unconventional Lessons*

Is there value to making lists? I think so. I make a lot of lists. Lists are motivating. They give us focus. They help remind us to get things done.

They also have the potential to be crazy making. Here is why: To-do lists are never empty. No matter how fast we work, or how diligent we are at crossing things off, the list is always full. There is always more to do.

Mathematically speaking, if a pail is never empty, what's the point of trying to pour out the water? What is the point of shoveling more and more dirt to fill a bottomless pit?

How can we ever be satisfied if our goal is to hurry through a list? If our goal is to try to get as much done as possible in a certain amount of time, it will never satisfy us.

The trick is to make a better list.

There are many theories and approaches to making good to-do lists and managing our time. My husband's favorite is the GTD (Getting Things Done) methodology by David Allen (www.davidco.com). Flylady.com is a popular website among homeschoolers. On this website, there are many practical ideas on how to keep organized and to get things done.

I have yet to meet an organizational method that wasn't effective in some way or another. But, no matter how good they are, none of them will work if we aren't filling our lists with the right things.

Tammy's four rules for making to-do lists for any time management system:

Quality. Fill it primarily with tasks that are both meaningful and enjoyable.

Balance. For every meaningful task on the list that isn't enjoyable, include one task that is enjoyable but meaningless.

Ownership. The person doing the task is the one who puts it on the list. I can't put a task for my kids to do, and they can't put one for me to do. We all create our own task lists.

Expectations. Never expect to get the entire list done. A homeschooler's "in-box" is never empty.

Before I came up with my new rules for making lists, this is what a typical day in my homeschooling mind was supposed to look like for our 7-year-old.

- **Monday**: Start work at 8:00am Math: pages 10-12 English read 20 min. and write a book report Health: read about digestion.
- **Tuesday**: Start work at 8:00am Math: pages 13-14 English read 20 min. and write in journal with a prompt Science: work in book pages 20-22
- **Wednesday**: Start work at 8:00am Math: pages 15-18 English read 20 min. and write a story with a prompt History: Read about Thomas Jefferson
- **Thursday**: Start work at 8:00am Math: pages 19-20 English: workbook pages 40-42 Drama class at 2:00pm.
- **Friday**: Start work at 8:00am Math: pages 21-24 English: workbook pages 43-45 Social Science: Workbook pages 10-12

This schedule seems pretty relaxed. I haven't even included P.E., foreign language, music, art, literature, religion or many other possible topics to cover. I decided that adding all of that extra stuff was going to be too overwhelming, so I kept our to-do list to the minimum that I wanted to get done everyday.

When I put this schedule together, I wasn't thinking about what my son would like. Nor was I thinking about my other two children. I was thinking of what would be a "good" well-rounded schedule for getting everything in. It looks good on paper. It looks doable.

However, my son didn't respond well to my idea of a good to-do list.

The tasks I listed were neither meaningful nor were they enjoyable for my son. I was the one who put meaning to the tasks. I didn't consider the tasks enjoyable either.

My son had no input in helping me put the schedule together. I was expecting him to follow a to-do list and schedule that I created for him. He had his own ideas of how to spend his day. Seeing that schedule, he was reluctant to include any kind of school work at all, let alone the pages I wanted him to do.

And finally, I was attached to the idea that these things absolutely had to be done. If we did these pages, he'd learn. When they didn't get done, I was annoyed. My son was annoyed if I made him do them.

All in all, this was a no-win schedule I created. I set myself up to fail. I was making the wrong kind of list.

I dumped the list, and dumped the schedule, and focused on my own personal to-do lists. After months of observation, listening, connecting discussion and trying out new things, we fell into a schedule that everyone was happy with.

Here's what our post-deschooling schedule looks like this month:

- **Monday**: We get up when we are ready. By 9 or 9:30, I start going around and shaking people to get up and enjoy the sunshine. By 10 or so, we're all hungry, so we gather ourselves up, and head to brunch. When brunch is done, we head to the library. 12:00 is guitar lessons for the oldest. The rest of the day is open.
- **Tuesday**: The youngest has a class at the park at 10. After her class, we go to lunch. The rest of the day is free.
- **Wednesday**: The day is free until 2, when all the kids have gymnastics. The little one has a class later on at 4:45. We relax in the morning knowing that the afternoon is full.
- **Thursday**: The youngest has a class at 10. The oldest has a science class at 3:30. We put lunch in between those classes somewhere.
- **Friday**: 1pm is piano lessons for the oldest. We usually have lunch out near his lessons beforehand. And sometimes we go to a nearby indoor playground and spend the whole morning there.

This schedule works great for us. Everyone worked together to make the schedule how it is. Everyone approves of the schedule. All the tasks on the schedule are enjoyable and meaningful. And lastly, everything is optional. Although we have the intention to get everything done, we don't have a problem skipping something to do something else.

Where's the schoolwork in all that? Where are the math, the reading, and the history?

Instead of assigning specific work on specific days, we have all the materials available for the kids. We have a general daily rhythm were the kids know they are expected to do some kind of schoolwork during the day. But they are the ones who decide when they will do it, and which subject they will cover.

We also have plenty of time in our schedule to take field trips, do an impromptu project, watch a video, play games, and many other outside-the-curriculum ways of learning. We fill our time with the things we like to do, and as a result. We end up doing all the subjects, but not necessarily in measurable increments.

How we fill in the blanks depends on a lot of things —none of which have to do with finishing a workbook, finishing a grade or trying to advance to the next level. All of our fill-in-the blank projects are derived by where the kids are at, and how they learn.

This sounds really lax and laid back. In a lot of ways it is. But I know my kids, because we take time to let them explore their interests and to fall into their own rhythm. Although they may not do all the projects I think are worthy, they work hard on the things they love to do. They work hard because their work means something to them. They get something tangible and meaningful out of what they do. I don't ask them to do things merely because it's on the list. I ask them to put things on the list, or we work together to put things on the list, that they have personal motivation to complete.

Finding Balance with a Schedule

In this new life away from school, waking up and doing…whatever…for the whole day can be panic inducing. We all have different ways of dealing with panic. Mine is to get out a piece of paper and make a list. Perhaps you might have had that experience.

I don't think we have to ever give up our lists, especially those who enjoy making them. Perhaps giving up schedules isn't necessary at all. Maybe, if we take a different approach to schedules, they can be a good tool for learning more about our children and ourselves.

Balance in our lives means that we don't have too much of one thing, while having not enough of another. Balance is why it's important to make sure we have time for fun every day, even if it's not on our list.

The following are four kinds of homeschooling plans that have worked for many homeschooling families. Adapt and modify as works for you.

The Big Idea Plan

> *"We almost always get to our goal through means other than the ones we put on our schedule. So why plan? Because people who don't make long-range plans seldom get to where they want to be. In short, a plan will get you to your goal but not in the way that's on the plan.*
>
> *So, plan. And, be prepared not just to change horses in midstream, but to change to a boat in midstream. Keep your goal, your Dream. Stay firm and fixed on that. Be prepared, however, for whatever methods come along to get you there. Especially methods not on your plan. Plan on it."*
> *- Peter McWilliams*
> *Do It! Let's Get Off Our Butts*

This first kind of planning is my favorite for when I'm feeling like I'm doing a good job getting the laundry and dishes done, but I'm not sure what our overall life purpose is. The big idea plan gives us a general direction, while avoiding stress that often comes with the hyper-focusing on the details.

Identify the biggest possible goal you can think of. For example, "Do more educational activities", "be healthier", "have a better relationship with the kids and spouse", "enjoy life more". Try tackling just one big goal at first, to see how it works.

Make a general plan for the day/week/month. Rather than make a detail plan of how to fulfill the big goal, create an open-ended one. Don't include numbers, time frames, rules or titles of books. If you have to squeeze those in there, keep it to a minimum, or give yourself lots of room for flexibility.

Examples of flexible plans for a 10 year old:

- This week/month: make time to read books out loud together. Mom or kids pick the book. Mom or kids read. Any topic, or level of reading, is OK.
- We also will include math, some examples of how this can happen are a grade 3 math book, a Sudoku book or playing a multiplication game outside, or any other place that math happens, try some new math games, ask if kids would like to play games. Check out the internet for some fun math games and learning ideas.
- Take a field trip. Some ideas are the children's museum, the recycling center and the farmer's market.
- Try some new recipes with the kids. Check out a book from the library about kids' cooking.
- See what kinds of books or videos they have at the library for art. Pick up some general art supplies at the dollar store.
- Dig out that old guitar we have, and mess around with it. Go to the library and see what kind of music books, CDs and videos they have. Look for classes or activities that involve music.
- Give daily hugs to kids. And listen to them to get cues to what they like and what might be something fun they'd enjoy.

After focusing on one goal for a while, it will become automatic, and won't need to be on the list anymore. Then it can be replaced with a new goal.

Every morning, review your plan carefully, then put it in your pocket and go about the day. This will give a certain focus to the day, and grounding, yet allow for space to let go and see how things unfold.

If panic sets in, pull out the lesson plan and look at what's written on the schedule. Just knowing you have something to fall back on is usually enough to reduce those panic attacks. It is our idea toolbox in our pocket.

Kids like to explore and discover. If we have our intention, with clear big goals, kids of all ages can be an integral part to how we fulfill those goals. They have the natural instinct to ask questions about the things they are interested in, and to know more.

The big idea plan gets us going in the right direction. When we are heading where we want to go, filling in the blanks happens as we go.

The "I'm Bored" Schedule

Most of us live in a world dominated by media, noise, people, entertainment and movement. It's rare to find time to just sit and do nothing.

Kids growing up in the kind of environment where things are always happening, there's always something on the schedule, always something slated for them to do, don't learn the fine art of sitting with themselves. At least not naturally. It takes effort to make time for quiet, retrospection, and being bored.

> *"Boredom will always remain the greatest enemy of school disciplines. If we remember that children are bored, not only when they don't happen to be interested in the subject or when the teacher doesn't make it interesting, but also when certain working conditions are out of focus with their basic needs, then we can realize what a great contributor to discipline problems boredom really is. Research has shown that boredom is closely related to frustration and that the effect of too much frustration is invariably irritability, withdrawal, rebellious opposition or aggressive rejection of the whole show."*
> *- Fritz Redl*
> *When We Deal With Children*

The purpose of the "I'm bored" schedule is to purposefully hold off on suggesting ideas of things to do, and let them get bored.

It's not a sign that we are a bad homeschooling parent if our kids are bored. Boredom is not always due to having nothing to do or not being stimulated enough. Sometimes, boredom comes from being so regularly *over*-stimulated, that our kids don't have any idea how to identify and take care of their own intellectual needs.

Allowing kids to get bored regularly, gives them three advantages:

- They learn to how to fill their time on their own, without being told what to do
- They turn to other activities that they would otherwise overlook
- They get a break from input, and time for their brains to relax

In our house, we have games, toys, books, art supplies, outdoor toys – essentially, lots and lots to do. And yet, there are times when the kids come to me and say, "I'm bored, there's nothing to do." How can there really be nothing to do? What they are really saying is that they don't have the tools to deal with being overwhelmed with all the stuff they have. Or, they are trying to tell me that they have a need for something, but they don't know how to fill that need.

Sometimes that need is, literally, for quiet, or alone time. Sometimes the need is to go outside and run around. Sometimes it's interaction with people. Sometimes it's sleep. The trick is to figure out what the kids really mean when they say they are bored, to help give kids the tools for figuring out their needs, and to help us identify what their needs are.

The way that the "I'm bored" plan works, is to have a non-scheduled, or loosely scheduled day, and refrain for making any suggestions or dictates on what the kids should be doing next.

Then, wait for the kids to get bored. Keep in mind, that being bored doesn't always manifest itself by a clear, "I'm bored, Mom." Sometimes it displays itself in the form of fighting, tantrums, destructive behavior, complaining, and sleeping when kids aren't tired. Your child might have other signs that he's bored.

When our children get bored, we are ready. We have an idea list with potentially interesting and meaningful activities all ready to go. This is part of our toolbox for dealing with boredom, and it can help us identify what our kids' needs are.

Here's a sample list:

- Clean out a closet, or the toy bin, or the arts and crafts drawer. Bringing stuff from the bottom of the drawer can stimulate new ideas, and distract the kids. Plus, it gets a drawer cleaned.
- Ask if the kids will help out with a chore that needs to be done.
- Go outside and work in the garden or have a picnic.
- Read a story out loud.
- Visit a friend, or invite a friend over.
- Sit and meditate or pray together.
- Start a household project like painting the walls, cleaning all the windows or getting rid of all the nasty stuff in the back of the fridge.
- Consider getting rid of stuff. Having less can sometimes be more. Also, getting rid of things makes for a simpler life, and helps us appreciate the things we have.
- Do workbooks, puzzle books, and read-alouds.
- Make cookies or bread.
- Write a letter to your friend, or Grandma.
- Watch an educational video or log into an educational website like http://www.pokemonlearningleague.com.

By bringing out the school work, project, or activity, the kids will either get really excited that they have something do to that isn't sitting around staring at each other. Or, they will suddenly remember those other projects they really wanted to do, and get busy. Either way, you all win. Whether they do the projects we want them to do, or whether they go off and create their own projects, they are learning.

The Everyone Pitches In Schedule

I like this kind of schedule because it requires a large amount of listening and communication skills to achieve.

This schedule is where everyone comes together and each person is allowed to add a pre-set number of items to the schedule, and that's it. That way, it's sure that every person is guaranteed to do a certain number of things they think are important, while allowing everyone else space to get their things done too.

How you do this is up to you. It could be a formal meeting, or a mealtime discussion, or something you put together one person at a time. It can work in many ways.

Make sure to set up some ground rules. For example, nobody can add an item to the list that requires other people to do work unless everyone agrees on it, or there is some other kind of negotiation (I'd like you to clean your room as one of my items. If you do that, I'll drive you to the skate park after book club on Thursday.)

Another ground rule could be that everyone gets a chance to speak, and when someone's speaking, everyone listens.

Lastly, for more fun and advanced schedule planning, give everyone a chance, at the end, to veto one activity, and negotiate for a replacement.

The end result will be a plan that everyone is happy with, and everyone feels responsible for keeping up.

A Descriptive Schedule

A descriptive schedule has worked great for many families I've talked to at conferences and online. It can also be called the "backwards" schedule. Instead of making a to-do list to follow during the day, try writing a description at the *end* of the day.

Start by observing what each person chooses to do, and when they do it. Also note how receptive they are to new ideas, classes, different types of activities and input at different times of day. After a few days or a few weeks, a pattern will emerge.

This is a great way to get a feel for what kind of educational and life schedule will work best with each person. It also gives us a chance to see just how much learning has gone on during the day without having to proscribe a learning environment.

It's OK if there doesn't seem to be a lot going on at first. After some practice, it'll get easier to notice the little things. If the child has been in a school a while, it may take him a while to figure out what his natural rhythm is. Or for that natural rhythm to settle in while his psyche and body get used to a new lifestyle. Be patient. This plan is a great way to get to know our children by honing our watching and listening skills, while putting away our judgments.

Letting Go and Holding On

The balancing act between letting the kids figure out their own rhythms, and giving them things to do to keep them from being bored, is tricky. A lot depends on the temperament of each family member, each person's learning style, and of course age and interests. There is also a huge difference between each family's cultures, and depending on what we find to be important, our definition of "balance" will vary.

It's also a balancing act to figure out how much of what we do in life and in education comes from what the kids want to do, and what the parents want to do. When we are in balance, things run along fairly smoothly. When we are out of balance, there can be arguments, frustration, and blaming. Someone isn't being listened to, or understood.

If we find ourselves out of balance towards the parental-direction side, we might notice that we interrupt what the kids are doing to get them to do other, more "important" things, like workbooks or something that's on our to-do list. We might find them refusing to do things we ask.

Before we stop what the kids are doing, we might want to ask ourselves, "What is the real reason that the kids have to stop what they are doing right now, and do one of these things on my list?" If the answer is "to keep me from having a heart attack", take a moment and ask yourself if you can see their current activity from a different perspective. What is it about the current activity that meets their needs? Why did they decide to do the activity they are in instead of something else? Is there a way we can both get our needs met right now?

The plans we make with the things we want to get done, and the things we want the kids to learn, are part of our toolbox for figuring out the direction we want to go with our family, and in life. When everyone is busy and happy, it means we are all doing the things that have meaning for us, and we are learning. The toolbox is for when we are sitting around staring at each other, and we are not sure what to do. Ah! We've got a schedule, a to-do list, an idea list! When the pressure's on, we've already done the thinking, so we can use the ideas we came up with before as part of our toolbox to move in a positive direction, when it seems like we are no longer doing so.

Kids Have Their Own Rhythm

After working on our schedule for a while, as a byproduct, I noticed that the kinds of things the kids learn in the morning are different than in the afternoon.

We all have natural rhythms in our life; when we like to eat, when we like to sleep, how long it takes us to wake up, when the best times of the day are, when we like to be social, when we like to be alone, and when we like to play and not have to think too hard.

In addition to have natural individual rhythms, every family has a rhythm that is created by the coming together of everyone's individual rhythms.

My oldest, for example, likes to play music all day – but his urge is at its height when he first wakes up and before going to bed. He prefers to read after lunch and when we're in the car. Playing outside is usually his favorite activity mid-afternoon, and after dinner. He likes to do puzzles, games, workbooks, and other focused activities when we are in the car and right before lunch.

This is an evolving process. But because I am aware of it, it's much easier to schedule things for him. I know that for the art class he had once a week in the spring, he needed to eat a sugar-free snack right before, even if he had a late lunch. The art class was only available right during the time of day his body wanted him to play outside. If I could get the kids to the park an hour before his art class, and make sure he has that snack, he was less likely to hop around and be noisy during art. But because I understand his schedule, I'm not surprised if he can't keep still for that hour.

Using a flexible or reflective schedule teaches us what these rhythms are when we don't have an external source controlling our lives.

When we use schedules to learn, rather than to dictate, they become tools that we can adjust to fit our needs. Schedules are not the enemy. Rigidity is. Adapt to a schedule that matches our temperaments and family rhythms, and we change our lives.

Hope's Story: *"We're new to homeschooling. My daughter is 8 and we had to pull her out of the public school system this year after the first 4 weeks. She was so stressed out over what had been going on at school that she wouldn't even look at a book. This was totally not my daughter. She's always loved learning, but this school is crappy, to say the least. (We moved to California a year and a half ago from Tennessee.)*

So I decided to send back the curriculum I'd purchased. I did some reading on "unschooling" and decided to give it a try. Basically, she went back on "summer vacation." I didn't push school or learning. We make frequent trips to the library, so she was doing plenty of reading. I just let her take a break.

That "break" lasted for about a month or so. She started getting bored and started dragging out old math workbooks and such and working in them. So I took that as a sign that she was ready to get started. I ordered an "easier" curriculum, mostly to help re-build her confidence. After it came in, she started working through it like crazy, and loving it.

I was very stressed out and a nervous wreck at first because I didn't know what was "right" or wrong. I've come to learn that there is no right or wrong way. Just let her find her way. I know that doesn't sound very clear, but it's true.

Emily is very much a self-starter. One thing I started doing with her last week is using a Goal Card. I write down what I expect her to complete on the following day. When she finishes each task, she draws a line through the box and moves on to the next thing. I rarely have to push her b/c once she gets started she doesn't quit until she's finished with all her work for the day.

Another thing I'm going to try is a rewards and demerits system. She loves responsibility because it makes her feel "big", so I try to incorporate that into her learning when possible."

Self Discovery Questions:

- When you have to get things done for yourself, do you tend to make yourself a detailed to-do list, a general to-do list with lots of flexibility, or none at all and focus on one project at a time?
- How about your spouse? What about your kids?
- Look at the patterns of everyone in the family – what are each individual's natural rhythms? What is the family's natural rhythm? Has it changed over the years?

Step 4: Teach Your Child As If No Other Exists

*"Education should be the process of helping everyone
to discover his uniqueness, to teach him how to
develop that uniqueness, and then to show him how to
share it because that's the only reason for having
anything. Imagine what the world would be like if all
along the way you had people say to you, "It's good
that you are unique; it's good that you're different.
Show me your differences so that maybe I can learn
from them." But we still see the processes again and
again of trying to make everyone like everybody else."*
- Leo Buscaglia
Love

A Culture of Competition

If you ask a teacher, or a parent, or anyone involved in education,
"What defines our current educational system?" the answer would
likely be "the standards". Educational standards are the stick by which
curriculum, success, rewards, evaluations, textbooks, tests, homework,
performance, and everything else done in school is measured by.

And certainly, they have their place there. Without standards, it's
difficult to assess the local schools, it's hard to get teachers and
schools to agree on what's important, and there is no way to know if a
child is "ahead" or "behind" among their peers. In a system with
thousands to tens of thousands of kids, using a checklist based system
to compare kids and schools and teachers to one another is arguably
the most efficient and "fair" way to go about it.

When we leave the system of school, all of the "good" that comes with the standards, loses its meaning.

You might find later, when you gain confidence in your ability to "see" your children outside of what everyone around you is trying to tell you about who they're supposed to be, the standards might play a part in what and how you decide to teach your children. But during the deschooling time, these standards are a distraction, and even a detriment. Standards-based learning requires that we look outside our family to define whether we are successful.

Where Do Standards Come From?

In a controversial and powerful article in the Feb/March 2000 issue of the Boston Review, Deborah Meier takes a close look at the purpose of nation-wide standards.

> "The current standards-based reform movement took off in 1983 in response to the widely held view that America was at extreme economic risk, largely because of bad schools. The battle cry—called out first in A Nation At Risk—launched an attack on dumb teachers, uncaring mothers, social promotion, and general academic permissiveness. Teachers and a new group labeled "educationists" were declared the main enemy, thus undermining their credibility, and setting the stage for cutting them and their concerns out of the cure. According to critics, American education needed to be reimagined, made more rigorous, and, above all, brought under the control of experts who—unlike educators and parents—understood the new demands of our economy and culture. The cure might curtail the work of some star teachers and star schools, and it might lead, as the education chief of Massachusetts recently noted, to a lot of crying fourth graders. But the gravity of the long-range risks to the nation demanded strong medicine."

In response to the perceived national educational crisis, rigorous national standards were born. Since then, they have been tweaked, reworked, reviewed and debated.

According to this same article by Meier, our current school standards have five main purposes:

- Pinpoint a single definition of what an educated 18 year old should be.
- Define who the authority is and who will make the decisions of what these goals are.
- Assessment of these authority-defined goals by a series of uniform tests.
- Enforcement by an authority that is far removed from application of said standards.
- Equity, so that all children will receive the exact same education.

None of these goals parallel goals that individual parents have for their children. In fact, homeschooling goals are quite the opposite:

- Allow our children to become educated adults around age 18 or so, in their unique way.
- Ultimately give the authority of learning and education to the person who is benefiting from the education—the child.
- Assessing the effectiveness of a child's education by their reactions to it.
- Remove enforced learning and replace it with opportunities to learn.
- An individual education based on a child's needs and interests.

The standards are created by two sets of data: general averages based on many variables, such as children's past performance, and what educators want and expect children to be capable of doing. There is a strong influence from special interest groups who demand that certain information be included (or not included) in the standards.

A fellow of the California Academy of Sciences, the president of The Textbook League, and the editor of The Textbook Letter, William J.

Benetta criticizes textbooks manufacturers for supplying "instructional products to American public schools [which] routinely cater to propagandists, respond to the propagandists' inducements, and turn out textbooks and other products which incorporate and endorse material derived from the propagandists' handouts. Any hustler, huckster, con artist, quack, or religious zany, if he has enough skill and money, can get his message into schoolbooks – or so it seems."

Standards are also used as a way to compare children to one another. Even if the standards were developmentally accurate (about which, there is much debate), they serve more as a comparing device than as a way to focus on the individual abilities and strengths of a child. If a child isn't performing at a certain level compared to the other students, standards allow teachers to identify where the child's perceived weaknesses are, so they can attempt to "catch up".

In a group setting, children are put into categories based on their abilities to make it easier to teach. These groupings also allow teachers to focus their energy on certain groups which will make the most difference in overall test scores. It boils down to a machine of efficiency. Assessing children solely on their own achievements is difficult and time consuming. Using standards in a group setting can appear to quickly streamline the effort to increase test scores.

For, example, in our current school system based on No Child Left Behind, the goal is to bring all children to an average reading level. If schools managed to bring more than ten or fifteen percent of the "underachievers" up to the middle, the bell curve would move up and there would be a new "average." No matter how much we push in school, or expect from the children, there will always be children who aren't developmentally ready to advance to the next level of thinking or ability. The focus on trying to get every child to be at least average in every subject is a mathematically impossible task. The only way to do that is to make sure that everyone is absolutely average. And since the push is so strong to bring kids up to average, that's where the focus is in our schools – make everyone average. That is decidedly not what we are trying to accomplish by homeschooling our children.

So, after knowing all of this, why would we ever use standards as a basis for teaching our children at home?

Mom, I'm not Standard

Our schools have become slaves to the standards, and by extension, so have the parents who send their kids there. Then, again by extension, so has our culture. Nothing else is more important in school than the emphasis on performing to the standards. Even when a child's individual needs are considered, whether or not that child needs help is decided based on whether a child is living up to the standards; each subject taught and how it's taught is determined by whether it covers something in the standards.

Homeschooling parents have good intentions by using the standards. We want to make sure that kids are consistently growing, and learning, and moving forward. But if we look at the standards, we have to be careful. Just like in schools, it can far too easily become yet another way to push kids to be like other kids, rather than being authentic.

When we are teaching at kids at home, comparing our kids to other kids, using the standards, or grading, or testing, is an easy way to lose sight of the freedom and flexibility we have to give our kids what they need when they are ready.

The Power of Saying "No" to Standards and Comparisons

Although I generally believe in moderation, there are times when we just have to say "no". Instead of spending the next few weeks or months wondering whether a child is reading at the same level as other kids his age, or whether he knows how to write neatly, or whether he has learned about the pilgrims, or Martin Luther King Jr., or any other thing kids are supposed to be learning by certain grades, focus on figuring out where your child is now.

Getting rid of the idea that we need standards, gives us freedom and power to better understand our kids.

It's a huge context shift – we are used to being told both as students and as parents, what to learn next. In high school, for example, we are told we have to learn biology first, then chemistry, and then physics. This ordering is based on a scientific study recommendation from 1890! It was around 1920 when high school science curriculum became as it is today. At that time, "biology" class included personal hygiene, sanitation, and food preparation. Yet, today, when biology has evolved into genetics, biochemistry and ecology, we still teach biology to high school students first, instead of physics and chemistry. When we depend on a system to tell us where to go next, little do we know how much of that content has been placed together because of outdated or arbitrary reasons.

Just like most of us don't know exactly what went into the food that is on our table, we know very little of what goes into making the standards. We assume that experts somewhere got together and used some kind of system to make the list of "important" knowledge that is taught in school. Yet, we judge our kids on how "good" of a student they are, based on one set of (often arbitrary) criteria created by means we are completely unaware of.

The children we are comparing to aren't even real. They are fictitious "perfect" children or "average" children. There is such a variance of what kids can do, that if we compare our children to anyone, there will always be places where our children aren't good enough. Or, if we are one of the "lucky" parents with kids who are ahead in every area, it's far too easy to say that our kids are "better" than the other kids (which, if we are comparing, then they are). I would argue that this isn't any more advantageous to a student than it is to be "behind".

By tossing the standards, we are saying, "What other kids are doing is not as important as what my kid is doing. Meeting him where he is at doesn't require that I know where other children are at too."

> **Kelly's Story**: *"My son, at the time we started homeschooling, was into Yu-Gi-Oh (having transitioned to that from Pokémon) and I choose to see it as a blessing in his life, not a curse to my pocketbook! As I was telling him he didn't have to do school the old-fashioned way, he asked if he could do a research report on Yu-Gi-Oh, expecting me to say, "No,"*

and thus showing my true colors. When I said, "If that's what you want to do," he got really excited and really went to town. In observing him, I saw that he knew how to research the way they taught in school, he just never had motivation to show it before. When he began to try and write a paper, I could see his energy dissipate; and I said, "You know, there is more than one way to present research. There are papers like you are working on, oral reports, computer presentations/slide shows, other kinds of graphic presentations, dramas...can you think of anymore?" He couldn't think of anymore but decided giving reports orally was a lot better than writing them down. Then he turned around to write again! So this time, I asked him if he would rather do an oral report than a written one. "I didn't think you'd let me change once things got started!" he replied. The next weekend, he proudly gave a 30 minute talk on Yu-Gi-Oh to me, his father, his sister, and his best friend. Then he wanted a grade, badly—so I gave him one.

We've gotten less "schooly" over the years, and I've brought my daughter home, too. Neither of the children think they have to have grades to prove they did something well. It's more like, "Did you enjoy it? Did you learn something? Do you want to learn more about it?" Instead of grading performance, we are teaching self-evaluation of important stuff: what do I like, I can learn new things, and I can do more if I want. We are very relaxed eclectic homeschoolers, and we have an absolute blast being with each other all day every day. Bringing them home was the best thing I could've done, since I couldn't start homeschooling from the beginning."

When we take on the responsibility to homeschool our children, we are making the statement that they are absolutely perfect the way they are now. There is nothing to "fix". There is nothing "wrong" with them. They might have no idea who they are, or they might not have enthusiasm for learning, but they aren't broken.

Where we go next, is entirely up to us. We are the ones who define our own success. We have the choice of what the criteria is for success.

A New List of Essential Learning

Everything we need to succeed in the world already exists in us. The word "education" came from the Latin word "educare," which means, "to draw out." Education isn't for putting things into our children's heads. It's for drawing them out to discover their own truth for themselves.

Essential learning boils down one simple set of information: Knowledge we need in order to survive.

Everything else we learn after that isn't essential, it is optional. It's not necessary to learn everything there is to know. In fact, that is a waste of time. Our time homeschooling is better spent on learning things that have meaning for us, make our lives better, and give us a satisfying life.

There is no way to determine what those things are going to be for our children. There are two ways to deal with the fear of not knowing what is going to be necessary later: we can make a list of everything that is possible to learn and try to learn it all "just in case", or we can wait until we need to know something, and learn it when it becomes necessary (or interesting).

Trying to learn everything is an inefficient way to educate kids; it's also ineffective. Our schools attempt to teach kids everything, yet nobody remembers everything they learn in school. Let's be optimistic and say, for the sake of argument, that we retain about 50% of what we are taught in school. That means that we forget 50% of thirteen years worth of material.

Why spend 50% of our homeschooling energy making sure that children learn things now so that they can later forget it? That time is wasted if our intention is to teach all of this material simply to cover the bases set by a list of standards.

Forgetting and Failure

Some would say that forgetting is a bad thing. I would argue that forgetting is part of the process of learning. Forgetting is only a failure if we have taken time to push through un-pleasantries in order to gain that knowledge.

If our learning process is enjoyable and meaningful, then forgetting is not a failure. It's simply a part of the learning process, and we are willing to take the time to learn it again if we need to later *because the first time we learned it was a pleasant experience.*

If we make learning an enjoyable experience, then we don't need standards. And we don't have to worry about failure.

Parents instinctually know that children are not failures. We know that if we took away the standards, took away expectations, and took away every judgment, every measurement and every outside influence of what and who our children are supposed to be—nothing is wrong with our child. Our child is perfect how they are right now.

Ann Zeise, the owner of A2ZHome'sCool and homeschooling veteran tells us about her perspective on working where our children are, instead of labels. "Your child is where he is, and you can only take him from there to where he wants to go. If you accept others' labels, you might miss something important. I did not learn to read well by the "Look-Say" method of my generation. I was put in the "slow" reading group as a first grader, and my parents were told not to have high expectations for me. Fortunately my parents threw that advice out the window! They signed me up for a children's book club and took me to the library often. My dad taught me how to use his drafting tools, and even bought me my own set. I think the two "lessons" I learned from my parents got me into webpage design and writing eventually."

When Standards Can Be Useful

Just like most any tool, the standards are not all bad. There is one thing we can use them for, if we are able to detach ourselves from the part where we feel required to do everything. We can use them as a source for ideas.

The first step to using standards in a non-intrusive, non-comparative way is to first avoid books that promise to help our child succeed in a specific grade. First, read books like *Discover your Children's Learning Style* and *In Their Own Way*, which are two examples holistic, long-term approaches to education.

Once we feel detached from the whole idea that kids can be divided up into grades and that they should be learning certain things at home because kids their age are in a certain grade, then we can take a peek at the standards.

And instead of looking at the standards as a checklist, look at it as an idea list. It's not a list of everything we have to do, but a list of things we can do.

If we can look at the standards and not feel compelled to act on them out of fear, pressure, or inadequacy, then they are safe to look at. If the standards give us heart palpitations – off to the storage unit they go (or the garage sale box) and it's time to reassess what our purpose is again, and why we are deschooling.

The Choice to Be Responsible

When we homeschool, we have a choice – we can control our tools, or they can control us. By deschooling ourselves from the grip of meeting the standards, we learn that we can live for a while without them. They are not required for deep learning, but rather one of the many tools we have available.

Standards do not tell us whether our children are learning. Nor do they tell our whether our children are going to be successful as adults. Only our children can truly know if they are getting what they need to be successful. Not being wrapped up in the constant evaluations and comparisons of school life, we can appreciate and nourish our children's authentic selves.

Nobody knows what's going to be important 20 years from now. Ann Zeise sums up, "Yes, small children need to learn the basics of math, reading, writing and speaking, and they need to read enough history not to repeat the mistakes of the past. They need to use the Scientific Method to solve real world problems they need to resolve. Beyond that, they need to learn to be good people, to create peace and harmony in the world and in the lives of the people they know and love. In no state content standards are you going to find peace, love, and harmony!"

The most important thing for us as homeschooling parents to learn is that school is not our master unless we choose it to be so. By changing how we look at the purpose and usefulness of school standards, we give ourselves the freedom to decide what is important and what isn't, instead of giving that privilege to someone else.

Self-Discovery Questions:

- What is your current perspective towards standards?
- Have you seen the standards for your child's grade level? How does looking at the list make you feel? Be honest to yourself about your relationship with the standards. Does looking at the standards (or even thinking about the concept of standards) make you feel inspired, enthusiastic, and encouraged? Do you feel indifferent? Or does it make you feel worried, like you aren't doing enough, and stressed out?
- If the idea of not looking at standards, or not considering standards, is scary, ask yourself why. What is it that standards provide that you feel you can't get elsewhere? What are standards for, in your opinion?
- How does the concept of "this is what other kids are doing" make your child feel? Does it encourage him to work harder, or does it make him feel deflated? Does the idea that he is behind or ahead of the other children affect how he learns?
- How much time does your child think about what other people are doing, and how much time does he appreciate his own achievements, independent of what others are doing? If other people succeed, or know the answer, does he feel dumb? If he knows the answer and others don't, does he think he's smarter? What do you feel about the concept of being "ahead" and "behind" on the effect it has on how children learn, and see themselves as learners?

Step 5: Creating Family Educational Goals

*"Having a philosophy is useless if it is simply an
awareness of rituals and the teachings of experts. To
make your philosophy work for you it must become
an energy pattern that you use in your daily life. It
must have both an eternal truth to it as well as a
utilitarian quality that makes you feel, yes, I know
this to be true because I apply it and it works."*
- Dr. Wayne W. Dyer.
Manifest Your Destiny

Best Homeschooling Practice

I'm generally wary of studies that tell me how homeschoolers "are".
Homeschoolers are generally hard to track, hard to categorize, and
vary significantly depending on the local community. Any study that
tells me what percentage of parents homeschool for religious reasons
or to help their child be more "advanced" might give me a vague idea
of what all homeschoolers across the country are doing, but it doesn't
give me a whole lot of information about our local homeschoolers.
Nor does it really make much of a difference for my particular family.
Everyone homeschools for their own reasons.

However, there was one study that caught my attention. And although
it's not a complete study by any means, nor does it prove anything
about the effectiveness of homeschooling compared to other kinds of
education, it gave me a huge boost in confidence about the choices
we're making for our family.

In 1993, Gary Knowles did an in-depth study of 53 adult
homeschoolers. They compared student "success" both academically
and socially. The kids were homeschooled with different kinds of
approaches; classical, curriculum-based, unschooling, unit studies,

"eclectic". Among the various people who participated in the study, there was no significant difference between their overall ratings of success. In fact, 90% of the respondents said they were satisfied with their educational experience.

Many studies have been done since then, and they continue to confirm this data. No matter what method, approach, or philosophy that the parents took, overall, homeschooled children tend to grow into successful and generally satisfied adults. What this means for you, is it doesn't matter how you homeschool, what method you use, what level of education you have or what your educational philosophy is, you're going to be fine.

These studies have reaffirmed my original idea that there is no universal "right" method out there to teach kids. None are automatically "better" than any other. Their answer is not in any particular method. The answer is in us.

Family First, Success Second

Numerous studies have shown that a child's success in school (based on test scores and grades) is highly correlated to the amount of parental involvement. The kind of parental involvement that is the most influential is outside of school, including doing activities together, working together on schoolwork, and a generally positive parental outlook that education is important and worthwhile. In addition, studies done by Brian D. Ray of the National Home Education Research Institute, and others, have shown that, unlike their public school counterparts, homeschooling students' academic performance is not related to family income, the degree of state regulation of homeschooling, teacher certification, the educational level achieved by parents, sex, or race (Brian D. Ray, 2005)

If all of these variables don't make a difference, how is it that homeschooled students tend to score the same, or better, on standardized tests than the average public school student? The only variable we have left is the same variable that makes school children successful in school and in life: family relationships.

The past four chapters have been about what to let go of – let go of curriculum, let go of workbooks, let go of schedules, and let go of standards. All of these things are what make schools today what they are. Black and white elements that can be measured, compared, organized, and equalized without any human contact whatsoever. It's time to let go of these objects that reduce the amount of humanity we share with our children. Depending on these objects makes us focus outside of our family relationships, and makes us worry that we aren't doing things right, fast enough, or good enough. These four elements of school make us doubt ourselves, make us dependent on an outside entity, and make us think that we don't know where we are going.

But, if we let go of all these things that we have been told by society, schools, parents, neighbors, friends, and politicians are the things that will bring us success – what do we use? What is there out there we can we find our grounding and strength with if not with a textbook or to-do list that clearly spells it out for us?

The first step to doing this is to know who we are, what we want, and where we are going. And doing it with the help of the only experts we really need – us.

Goal Setting, Family Style

Creating family and educational goals is the first step to this rediscovery. A family educational plan reflects your beliefs and abilities, gives you direction and opens up the opportunity for us to live with integrity. When we live what we believe, we can say, "I know why we are doing this, and I know what it means to be successful. I am confident that we are doing what works best for us. And we're willing to be honest with ourselves about what it takes to be successful."

Family-based educational goals are a broad view of learning. Once we know what our overall goals are, it's easier to find what works for us. In addition, we can avoid the trap and distraction of the overwhelming collection of learning resources being marketed to us. Putting our family's needs first means less tears, less frustration, and a lot of good memories.

Putting together our family-based educational goals, and then using them in our homeschooling lives, can be divided into four steps:

- Define your family goals
- Define your educational goals
- Come up with your own definition of success using these goals
- Create a measurement to know when things are working, and when they aren't

Your family has its own distinct personality. Are you the kind of family who likes to joke with one another, hang out at the park and throw a ball around, or stay up late and get up late? Do you prefer to sit quietly and read together, have subtle communication with one another, or leave little notes in each other's books? Do you have a favorite activity that you do together, such as horseback riding, music, video games or camping? Are you generally high energy, low energy, or do you go back and forth? Some families are very predictable, some aren't. Some families put spirituality and religion at the forefront, some have it as a backdrop, and some don't find it very important. Some families like a lot of technology in their lives, others prefer being in nature most of the time (and others like a mix of both). Every family is unique.

Take a moment to reflect on these questions: What is it that makes your family unique? What is your family's personality? If someone were to describe your family as an outsider, what would their impression be? What do you want their impression to be? If you could boil your family philosophy down to one sentence, what would it be?

The answers you come up with give you a platform from which all other educational decisions can evolve. When we know who we are as a family, we are able to see clearly whether the activities and approaches we take, or our children take, are a good fit for us. When a family has a well-defined set of family goals, it's easier to see when something is working with those goals, or against them.

Strategies for Defining Family Goals

There are many ways to figure out one's family goals. The exact protocol for coming up with a common set of goals is ultimately up to you. The only essential element is open communication where everyone ultimately feels like his or her perspectives have been heard.

Family Meetings

One of the more formal ways of creating and maintaining family goals is to hold regular family meetings. For many families, especially those with really busy schedules, carving out time for family meetings is a great way to stay in touch and keep the lines of communication strong.

Family meetings can connect us, while giving us all a chance to voice our concerns, preferences and things that have worked for us. If there is a lingering issue, or a lack of cohesion, making special time to come together as a family can provide a venue to find solutions. Meetings are also a good time to give each other undivided attention.

General Tips for Successful Family Meetings

- Set a date and time when everyone's available, and mark it on the calendar
- Treat it as a special time to connect, not a time to fix problems
- Focus on creating common goals
- Allow everyone time to speak. Some families use a "talking stick". The person with the talking stick can't be interrupted. If someone has something to say, they have to wait until it's their turn with the talking stick.
- Open the meeting with something positive, such as hugs, everyone saying what their favorite family activity is, or an inspiring poem.
- Remember your established family goals

The concept of family meetings is not new. Many family support networks suggest them for conflict resolution and family closeness. Some find making family meetings to be as important as scheduling vacations. When we are homeschooling we might get the impression that we are "connecting" simply because we are around each other a lot. It's also easy to get distracted by life and so forget to have "deep" conversations. Or to give our kids lots of kudos and hugs. Family meetings can be our chance to make the conscious effort to connect with each other.

Informal Family Meetings

If formal meetings don't fit your family's personality, consider having regular informal family discussions.

I find this works well when one family member is interested in these kinds of meeting of the minds, but the rest of the family is resistant to the idea of formally talking about important issues.

A family meal is a perfect place for an informal meeting. Talking while on a walk or during a long car ride are also activities that provide opportunity to connect with one another. Using the same tips as above, family goals can be established and discussed in a less structured way, and still arrive at the same goal: to come to a consensus about what you family's philosophy is and to make sure that everyone's opinion on what's important is being heard.

We evolved into our regular family meetings because our extended family lives about an hour away. The many drives we have taken to see them have provided the perfect time for us to talk about what education, and family, mean to us. My husband and I talk about what kind of parents we want to be, what we feel is important for our children to know, and what our family's personality is. We are casual about it, just bringing up what's on our minds, but the essence is the same as a family meeting: we all want to know what it means to live in this family, and what we stand for.

During these rides, our kids can hear everything we talk about. Sometimes they pipe in with a comment, but mostly, at the ages they are at, they listen. We ask the kids sometimes, too, what they think about our discussion. When they have an opinion, it's time to listen and take them seriously.

Over time, we have all learned that it's safe to bring up grievances and safe to talk about "issues". They don't fester, and we continue to understand each other, even as we evolve into more mature, experienced and complex people.

Family Check-ins

Another option to the formal or informal "meeting" is a family check-in. If everyone is open and willing to connect on a regular basis, it doesn't take lot of effort to do a quick catch-up of where everyone is. We can keep abreast of what everyone is doing, what's important to them, and where they want to go next. These check-ins can be done anytime; while picking someone up from a class, during commercials between shows, while playing a game together, when saying "good morning", or while watching the kids play in the back yard, for example.

However you decide is the best way to stay connected with your family, listening to our children and our spouses in this way gives us insight on what is working, and what isn't. The things that are working get a positive response, the things that aren't, get a negative one. When we meet as a family, the goal becomes about getting everyone's needs met. It also makes it less likely that one person is deciding on what everyone should be doing, and trying to figure out a way to make everyone comply. Getting everyone's opinion and perspective is the first step to knowing whether what we're doing is "right". It's the first step towards empowering ourselves to use our own needs and direction to figure out which educational tools to use. It's the first step to becoming confident in our own educational choices.

Why Family Meetings Work

Between these car rides, and our many other conversations we've had as parents, and as an entire family, we have created what is the Takahashi style of living. You'll find, as well, that your family discussions and homeschooling experience will evolve you into your own style of living.

In a way, my family is lucky, because I've been forced by circumstance to pay a lot of attention to this phenomenon. Due to my work as a homeschooling and life learning writer and activist, I have to think hard about "how we do things" in order to be able to write my articles. I have to listen closely to what my children and husband say, and notice their perspectives on things that happen around them in order to portray a fair representation of who they are to the public. Because I have chosen a career that puts me in a spotlight position, I need to be extra careful to live up to what I've declared as important in my writings.

Through this experience as a writer and speaker, and talking with hundreds of other homeschooling families, both new and veteran, I've come to this conclusion: Those who are clear about their family goals, who have a family consensus on what those goals are, and who talk about those goals regularly, are more successful and happy homeschoolers.

It doesn't matter what those goals are, so long as they exist and they are clearly displayed on the table where all family members can see them, and can have a fair say on whether they agree with them.

The reason this is so important, and so integral, to a successful homeschooling life is because we are challenged to live up to what we believe. When we put our ideas and truths out into the world, we are much more likely to live those truths. We become a family of integrity, by being honest and accepting with each other, and with ourselves.

When our ideas of who we are, and what we believe in, are not just in our heads, but shared with our entire family, it his harder to "cheat" and ignore our own incongruent behavior. People notice when we aren't living what we believe.

And when we aren't living what we believe, we can ask our family for support in helping us live that, or to redefine who we are to reflect reality and what works.

Coming to a Consensus

"I encourage you, kids and parents, to all start keeping lists of what your feel are important skills to have, and important qualities to integrate into our personalities. I can almost guarantee that the list will look a whole lot more like the Boy Scout Laws than any state content standards: trustworthy, loyal, helpful, friendly, etc."
- Ann Zeise

One day, I was writing a blog post about the importance of family goals. My husband and I had talked about our goals many times, but I had never taken the time to write them down, so it was fairly easy to make my list. But after I made the list, and saw them in print, in my own words, I felt this overwhelming pride and security. I said to myself, "Not matter what happens in our world, if we keep these things true, we will have done a good job as homeschooling parents."

The Takahashi List of Family Goals

- To respect ourselves, and the people around us
- To use negotiation to get our needs met
- To show empathy towards others
- To lead a life of simplicity
- To give people space when they need it
- To live authentically and let others do the same
- To listen to one another, and take each other's words seriously
- To be forthright in our speech, but to also hold on to words that are hurtful

- To help others as a matter of practice
- To know and appreciate ourselves
- To stand up for ourselves without hurting others
- To put relationships first
- To recognize that everything we do is a choice we made.
- To accept responsibility for our choices without guilt and to act responsible
- To appreciate life in the moment
- To avoid judgment as much as we can, and to find a way to see the good in our experiences

Our goals don't say how we are going to get there. They portray the values and goals that are so important to us that we put them first, before anything else. Period. Because these goals are imperative, they become the basis for anything else we do: work, play, relationships and education.

Tips for Making a Family Goal List

- Keep the goals simple and broad.
- Only add goals that everyone agrees on.
- Leave room to amend, add or remove goals as life evolves.
- There are no right answers – don't worry about what people will think of your goals.
- Include only goals that define your family, not goals that you think you're supposed to have.
- Include only goals that make you feel good. Don't add goals that make you feel guilty or frustrated.
- Define any terms that might be ambiguous.
- Avoid judgment terms like "good", "fair", "right".

Our family goals are important because they are the basis for the next set of goals we are going to make: our educational goals. Our understanding of what we value in life, gives us a tool for figuring out what education means to us. "Education" is a term that cannot be universally defined. The individual himself can only define what constitutes a "good education".

This is where family goals come in: When we know what we want out of life now, we are teaching our children how to identify what they want out of life too. We are providing a foundation for their educational life with a solid family life.

Whichever method of family communication you prefer, I encourage you to answer the 'big" questions of life and family: Who are you? What is important to your family? What is your idea of a "good" family? Where do you want your family to be, if you could have it any way? What makes you, and all the individuals in your family, truly happy and satisfied? Come up with a list of qualities that everyone agrees on, which represent your family.

Then post them on the wall, or on the fridge, and remember; this is what your family is about. Decide to make choices that honor that. And when others don't make those choices, be understanding and loving, remembering that you are all living together. It takes time and practice to learn who we are.

Defining Our Educational Goals

Educational goals are an important guiding element to our home-schooling journey. Using our family goals as a guide, we can create educational goals that are in congruence with what we value and who we are. Instead of waiting for someone else to tell us what is important to learn, we have the roadmap right in front of us.

During your family meetings, once you have your family goals established, take some time to talk about educational goals. Work together to make a list of things that are important to each of you. On this list, anything is fair game. Big ideas, small ideas, today's goals, tomorrow's goals, anything.

In the beginning, you might find yourself rewriting your goals often. Even now, after years of homeschooling, I still rewrite our goals every regularly. I love to see where we are headed. I like having the list in front of me, to remind me what it is that really means something in learning. Re-writing my list of goals every so often reminds me of what's really important.

But also, we are always changing. As we change, our goals change. What we want out of life changes, and who we are changes. In the beginning of our homeschooling journey, we did quite a bit of evolving. As a result, I made a lot of educational lists (both in my head and on paper). I would make a list, then I'd get input from another family member, which would turn my list of goals on its head, and I'd have to start over.

It was part of the adaptation process for all of us. And it was an important part. Having the list of goals got us through times when we were worried or scared. It reminded us of why we made our decision in the first place, and helped us focus on what was important to us, rather than letting our minds wander on how we might be messing up.

Our educational list helped us focus on what was *right*, rather than worry about what was wrong.

The Takahashi List of Educational Goals

- For everyone to be honestly successful in their day to day lives, and to have confidence that they will continue to have success no matter what paths they choose
- For everyone to have the knowledge of how to obtain information, who to ask for help and to be confident enough to pursue knowledge in their own way
- For everyone to love learning, whatever that may be
- For everyone to be the person that they are, and receive unconditional trust no matter where their interests and personalities take them
- To make sure that everyone has a sense of pride in who they are and in what they've done. This leads to a life of integrity
- For everyone to genuinely love to be alive

When I'm frustrated, or feeling like I'm not doing enough, I look at my list and ask, "Are we living a life that parallels our vision of what education is for? Do we all agree that these are our goals?" If two people are not in agreement about whether one of the goals is worthy of considering, then it creates friction. The list has to be unanimous. Even if it's a short, short list, there has to be universal agreement that we all believe in certain things in this family. It doesn't mean that we can't change our lists. It doesn't mean that we can't make exceptions.

Two common problems during deschooling can be solved with a list of educational goals.

- Kids "hating" learning
- Parents not understanding why kids don't take learning seriously

One of the reasons kids get so frustrated in school is because nobody is listening to them. They are being asked to learn under someone else's list of educational goals. They have no say in that list, and they have no idea what that list is. Kids can also be burned out by the fact that the list is so long and specific that it seems like no matter what they do, they can't possibly ever comply with all the goals.

It takes time and experience for them to re-learn what it means to get an education. This is where your list of educational goals can help children or teens learn that they are being listened to, they can indeed learn, and that they are fully capable of being successful. Being a part of making this list will give them confidence that they can define for themselves what learning is, with your help and support.

Parents can also get frustrated with kids who shut down or seek out escapist activities. By including their children in the process of creating educational goals, parents can learn to trust their children and see how their children do indeed take learning seriously, but that that they need to have some autonomy and inclusion in the process.

In addition to having the experience of letting our children have autonomy, we parents can also find our own success by using family-created educational goals to support our children. Supporting our children is one of the most satisfying aspects of being a parent. We can use our thoughtfully created educational lists as a tool to learn how to be a better parent to our children.

Happy children have a meaningful, interesting and balanced life. They don't need a life where "nothing bad ever happens", but a life where they feel strong, able to take risks, recover from failure, recover from trauma if it ever happens to them, and know they have a solid sense of community and family. I think we can all agree that we want our children to never lose interest in learning and growing, to be interested in the world, and to know who they are. We want our children to grow up and not worry about what will make them successful, because they have learned how to be successful by living a childhood full of chances to define their own success. Being cognizant of our entire family's educational list helps us achieve that.

Making Use of Educational Goals

When we make decisions about which classes to take, which books to use, how much time to spend on this or that, what to *do*; our educational goals are the guide. Does what we are doing, or what we are planning, move us toward these goals? If not, why not? What's missing? What could be different? Perhaps, we are going in the wrong direction? Or are we trying to go too fast? What choices can we make that are parallel to our goals?

Now, we are empowered. Having clearly outlined our own goals, we don't have to rely on anyone else's idea of a good education. We *know* what a good education is. A good education is one where our educational goals and our family goals are met.

When we are working with our children, knowing our educational goals gives us the power to let go of things when they aren't working, and move on to something else with confidence. Without these goals, we could easily push on with something that's not working, because we aren't thinking about the bigger questions. It's too easy to get caught up in the details, to be a slave to a curriculum or what's supposed to be a tool for learning, when we don't know what we are educating for in the first place.

Asking, "Why is this so important?" eventually leads us to a core reason, a basic tenet, that we're making our decisions on. Asking "why" until we get to the core value, makes us see when what we are doing doesn't fit into our goal system at all. If something isn't working, odds are, we haven't asked "why" enough times, and something we are choosing to do is clashing with one of our family member's idea of what's important. It's time ask "why" until we've gotten to the core issue, and deal with that.

One of the things I decided early on as a parent, then as a homeschooler, was that everything I asked my kids to do, and everything I demanded of my family, had to have a reason that I could explain. If I had to resort to, "because I said so" or to "because that's how it is," then I needed to rethink why I was asking something. As a thinking homeschooling parent, I look at my responsibility to be a role model to my kids to teach them how to think and express ideas. If I can't even identify why they *need* to do their workbooks, or *need* to take a class, or *need* algebra, then how can I teach them to identify in their own lives when they really need something? How can they know the difference between what they really need to do, and what other people think they need to do?

But, I've learned, I have to be careful not to over-explain. When we over-explain, kids stop listening. When it might seem to me that I'm explaining all the various reasons why my kids need to comply with me right now, the kids hear "yap yap yap". It's not that they are being lazy or impetuous. Have you ever had someone over-explain something to you when they didn't like what you were doing? It gets to a certain point where we have to turn off our ears and crawl into our hole to protect ourselves. The other way to handle the situation is to fight back.

When our kids shut off, or fight us, it is a clear indication to us that we are doing something that they need to protect themselves from. Whether we are "right" or not, we have to make a decision right then – is this meeting our family or educational goals? Then, we have to ask "why" until we get to the core issue. Which family or educational tenet are we fighting for? And, do we both agree on this goal?

It's important to know why we are making a choice. Explaining our motivation to our kids why we want them to do things should encourage them to keep asking "why". The reasoning we supply to them should be clear, make sense and take into account their feelings and needs as well. If we do this consistently, we are teaching our kids that it's safe to stand up for themselves in the world and speak honestly about the world they live in. They will have learned to trust us, because we have a history of giving them a real, solid answer, which we don't punish them (with moods or attitudes) for wanting to know.

Our role isn't just to teach children *stuff*, but to teach them to know themselves, to understand that they create their own lives, and to look at the bigger picture. To see the world as a place of discovery, options and possibilities – not just one set of rails with 10 foot walls on each side. Putting educational goals into practical use, by working with our children to make choices with integrity together teaches them far more than any stuff they can ever learn – it teaches them how to learn.

Your family goals define your homeschooling. Not what someone else's educational goals are. Not the school's, not the government's, not the neighbor's, not society's, but your family's. The world can give you ideas and perspective – but the end result is up to you. Rebelling simply for the sake of rebelling isn't helpful. But don't be afraid to say "what everyone says is right, just isn't right for us." And then decide what is appropriate for you with empowerment. Don't be mean about it. Don't get angry for people trying to push you their way. It's human nature. Simply say, "Thank you for your advice, I'll take it into consideration," then go back to your core family and educational values to make your ultimate decisions.

Making a clear list of what we need from education empowers in another important way that is often overlooked. It helps us keep from being overwhelmed by choices. When you know what your family's educational goals are, facing a room or catalogue full of curriculum won't be intimidating. Instead of approaching the world's thousands of options for educational materials, you'll be discerning. You will already have your method, your direction. Instead of being the homeschooler looking for a curriculum, you'll be the satisfied homeschooler willing to settle for nothing but the very best.

Curriculum and other kinds of educational material become your tools and toys, not your lifeline.

Learning Styles

In the early 80's, Howard Gardner and David Kolb were two of the first to formally introduce a system of learning styles, or, as Howard Gardner called them, multiple intelligences. Being aware of learning styles or multiple intelligences is an important part of being able to work your educational goals around everyone in your family.

The basic premise of learning styles is this: everyone has a different preference for how they process information. *Discovering Your Child's Learning Style* Mariaemma Willis and *In Their Own Way* by Thomas Armstrong are two of my favorite books on the subject.

According to Thomas Armstrong, there are seven styles of learning: linguistic, logical-mathematical, spatial, musical, bodily-kinesthetic, interpersonal and intrapersonal. Mariaemma Willis's book has an in-depth test that you can take to find out how your child prefers to learn. Both Armstrong and Willis emphasize that everyone can and does learn with all seven styles, but, some are easier and more effective than others.

Although I don't like to categorize people, or focus too much on labels, I found thinking about learning styles help me see my kids from a much larger perspective. Which ultimately led me to the conclusion that if our kids aren't learning something, it might be that they don't like *how* the material is presented.

We've all heard of kids saying, "I don't want to." "I'm bored" "I hate math." Your own kids might have said something similar. So much of what we see as educational problems is adults not being able to truly recognize, or admit, that everyone has a different way to learn. Or, if we do recognize it, we have no way to adapt to it.

Perhaps the easiest way to understand this is to look at our own style of learning, and that of our close friends and family. People who have already been through school and are now adults. What inspires different people to learn new things? What are their learning styles?

I encourage you to do some research on learning style, then come up with your own learning style profile. After you've done yours and a few close friends or family, then think about our children.

Not all "learning styles" are academic. Think of things like:

- What is your daily learning rhythm like? When do you like to work, think, play, rest, and "veg"?
- Do you prefer to talk, think, or do?
- Would you rather read or listen to new information? Or maybe you'd rather have a conversation about it?
- Do you take more in when your eyes are closed, or open?
- Do you like things planned out, or spontaneous?
- Do you like to "wing it" or follow a recipe?
- Do you read the instructions when you are building something?
- Do numbers, sequences and logic come naturally to you? Or do you see things like one big story? Or maybe you see things in colors, images and descriptions?
- Do you remember names, places, and personal details easily? Do you remember what you did and how you felt better?
- Do you prefer talking about the big picture of a problem, or focus one detail after another?
- Do you like to see all sides of an issue, or do you prefer to find the one side that works then ignore the rest?
- Do you prefer to keep looking for a better solution when you've found a satisfactory one? Or do you stop once things are "good enough"?
- Where do you get your inspiration?
- Do you prefer to do things in small sections over a course of hours, days, or weeks? Or do you prefer to do projects all at once?
- Do you prefer to do tasks that are clearly easy to do, or do you prefer challenges?
- Does it make you nervous to try new things?

- Does it frustrate you when you have to do the same thing over and over?
- If you picked up a book on "how to make your house look marvelous," do you feel compelled to start from the beginning and read every word, or do you skip forward to the parts that seem the most interesting or helpful?
- Do you prefer to be alone when you are doing a project? Or do you like a group?
- When you have a problem that you don't understand, do you feel compelled to ask someone right now to find out the answer, or do you put it aside and wait until inspiration hits?

On the other side, don't get too attached to the idea of learning styles. Our kids are complex people. All this is to get us thinking about our kids, not to find another way to label them. Knowing that learning styles exists opens up a whole new world of accepting our kids for who they are. It also gives us another good reason to let them have a say in their own learning goals. Getting input from them about what and how they want to learn is the best way out of them all to discover our children's learning styles. And it's the best way to find the most effective way to teach them.

What Is Success?

Undoubtedly, we all chose to homeschool for some reason related to the success of our children. Perhaps we want them to have the ability to follow their interests, to have less stress, to have more options, to live more spiritually, or to go at their own pace. Whatever our reasons were for deciding to homeschool, we can all agree that success played a huge part of that.

But what does success mean exactly?

> *"I've always told people that to be successful you have to enjoy what you're doing and right now I really enjoy what I'm doing. I'm having too much fun with my life. Why would I want to do something else?"*
> *- Donald Trump*

"One should guard against preaching to young people success in the customary form as the main aim in life. The most important motive for work in school and in life is pleasure in work, pleasure in its result, and the knowledge of the value of the result to the community."
        - Albert Einstein

"To laugh often and much; to win the respect of intelligent people and the affection of children...to leave the world a better place...to know even one life has breathed easier because you have lived. This is to have succeeded."
        - Ralph Waldo Emmerson

"Success is going from failure to failure without losing enthusiasm."
        - Winston Churchill

In my personal and professional research into what constitutes homeschooling success, I have found that across the board, the true definition of success is that people are satisfied with their lives and genuinely like who they are.

Every other variable, such as a job, money, relationships, hobbies, or time, were personal manifestations of success, not the definition of success in and of itself.

What this means is that any detail that we consider successful is a personal opinion of our definition of success. Every single person has a different idea of what success is.

Now, if everyone has a different idea of success, how can we possibly make a universal construct of the path to success? Well, we can't, of course. But that's exactly what schools, curriculum and even society, attempts to do – to say that there is one path that will unilaterally create success.

The way to success is to not only redefine what success is, but to give every individual the space and opportunity to create their own definition of success.

Success comes in so many different forms and flavors, that we can't identify it from the outside. Knowing we are successful can only come from the inside. Nobody anywhere can accurately define success for us. Translate this to a homeschooling situation, and we then can see how telling to tell our children what they need to do to be successful, won't work. All we can do is help them discover for themselves what makes them successful, and support them in that search.

The tools we have to help them do this are recognizing everything our children need right now to be successful. Having created our family and educational goals together gives us insight on how we can do that.

Conversely, the more space we give our kids to be successful, the wider the door is open for our kids to fail. But as Winston Churchill so wisely observes, failure is an essential part of achieving success. Without failure, we can't learn.

How can you help your kids achieve success and learn from failure? Do your educational goals leave room for your kids to define their own success and to safely experience dealing with failure?

Determining If Our Goals Are Working

Now that we have family goals, educational goals, and our own definition of what success is, we can determine if what we are doing is "working". If what we are doing fulfills our family goals, fulfills our educational goals, and creates an environment where everyone is able to create their own success, then yes, it's working. When we are worried about things being too "easy", or not doing enough, we can look at these criteria to redirect us, calm our fears, or inspire us.

If we find ourselves getting stressed easily, or bickering about the same topic repeatedly, it's time to look again at our goals and view of success, and see which part of these things aren't being satisfied. We might need to change a goal, try a different approach, or simply listen to each other more, to see where the source of our frustration is coming from.

When what we are doing is in line with what we really believe to be the meaning of education, of life, and of what success is, things are easy. When what we are doing isn't in alignment, then it is stressful.

"Hard work" is a misnomer. We, as a society, think that hard work is synonymous with stress or unpleasantness. But we've all done hard work that was enjoyable. When we are doing work that is meaningful and interesting, time can fly and we can push through difficult tasks easily. Some call it being "in the zone" or "in the groove." In 1975, Mihály Csíkszentmihályi, a psychology professor at Claremont Graduate University, proposed the existence of this state, and called it "flow". He has written many books on the subject, including, *Flow: The Psychology of Optimal Experience*, published in 1991.

Csíkszentmihályi's book is one of many which discuss this "optimal" state. Due to the great achievements and personal fulfillment that the state of flow creates, it is of great interest to schools and businesses.

The Commonly Observed Elements of Flow

- Clear self-aligned goals
- A high degree of concentration that is hard to disengage from
- Absence of self-consciousness
- Time disappears
- Direct correlation between ability level and challenge
- A sense of personal control over the situation or activity
- The activity is intrinsically rewarding

Children and people who are able to regularly work in this state of flow feel good about the work they've done, and are able to make great strides in learning and achievement.

This is one of the reasons that educating our kids can seem "easy" and still be full of hard work. If we are in flow regularly, our hard work fits in our lists of goals and is right at the level of what our brains are ready for. If it does, it'll seem much "easier". The more we can provide that space for our children to learn, the more often they will be able to reach a state of flow, the more often we'll feel like homeschooling is "working".

One of the most important jobs of a homeschooling parent isn't to teach topics, but to know our children. Our job is to be able to decipher their needs, their perspectives, and to see it from their point of view. The best kind of education we can give them is to help them achieve their goals. The way we teach, what we teach, and how we go about being a parent to them are all tools for the big picture – creating a family of people who are successful, confident and authentic.

Fellow homeschooler, Leslie, has been homeschooling for eight years, and has two boys, 11 and 13. She told me her story about what she would have done differently if she were to start over.

She said that playing with her children, using the low-cost math, spelling, and grammar books she picked out in the beginning, and journaling daily, were positive choices they made in the beginning of their journey.

She also mentioned the importance of hosting events at her house. Many homeschoolers wonder where to go to learn together in a group, such as classes or parent-driven group activities. Inviting people to her house to work together on a project was an effective out-of-the-box solution. She was lucky to have found this solution early on, and continues to host events and classes at her house today.

Of the things she said she would do differently, relaxing topped her list. She would have gone back and spent more time enjoying the presence of her children, rather than worrying about what they were missing. She also mentioned how she had joined co-ops for the purpose of socializing, rather than joining the groups her children were interested in. She realized that the benefit of "socialization" was negated when the kids weren't all that interested in the group.

Her last word was to warn us from buying too much curriculum in the beginning, and not to worry so much about getting it all done. Do the best, she suggested, and leave the rest.

Leslie's experience is not uncommon. Many long-term homeschoolers offer a similar kind of advice. Even so, I can hear this kind of story a hundred times, and still benefit from the reminder that education is about the kids, not about what we "should" be doing to reduce our own fears. It's a life-long learning experience that starts in this moment, of discovering who we are and how we learn.

Self-Discovery Questions:

- What are your life goals as a family?
- What are you educational goals as a family? What are your educational values?
- If you had to give up everything else, what would be the most essential values and goals that are worth fighting for, no matter what?
- Which decisions have you made recently that weren't in line with your family goals? Which ones were in line with your goals and values? What were the results of these decisions and what did you have to give up to make them?
- What percentage of your decisions are made from fear of what other people will think over what the people in the family will think and feel?
- Who is has the most influence on your educational and family decisions? Is this influence supportive and strengthening or does it create friction in the family?
- If you could have one thing be right and true about your educational life, what would it be? What are some steps you can take to move toward that vision?

Step 6: Get Hooked Up, Get the Kids Hooked Up

*"The idea of learning acceptable social skills in a
school is as absurd to me as learning nutrition from a
grocery store."*
        - Lisa Russell

*"Friendship is born at that moment when one person
says to another, 'What! You too? I thought I was the
only one"*
        - C.S. Lewis

What Resourceful Homeschoolers Know About "Socialization"

OK, we've got to talk about this. Socialization.

How in the world do we meet people when our kids don't go to school?

When parents drop their kids off at school, it provides a pre-established meeting ground for kids and parents. Whether or not that meeting place is healthy or desirable is not generally brought to question. What's more important, is that there are a lot of people congregated at this one place called school, and they all have one common experience together—being parents of kids in that school.

Having this one thing in common gives them all a reason to need or want to talk to one another. To share advice, stories, information, and offer help. With this system in place, parents, and kids, don't have to look elsewhere to find friends or support. Some kids do make friends outside of school experience, but the overall system is set up so that people don't have to learn how to make friends anywhere except for in school.

School is an easy way to be social. It requires no forethought, no research, no effort, and no risk. Someone else provides the setting, the reason to be there, and a time and place to meet. School is a common tie between parents and between kids, creating a community where none existed before. And none of the parents or kids has to do anything, at all, to create this environment. It's handed to them, for free even.

Most of us grew up with absolutely no training or experience in making friends in the real world. Not only is deschooling about becoming experienced in learning outside of the school system, it's also a quest to learn how to teach our kids to have a relationship with people in the world around us on our own terms.

In our culture, we are taught from an early age that friends are supposed to be handed to us. We have no idea how to go out and meet people!

This fact is never more obvious to me than when people honestly wonder how a homeschooler can possibly make friends without the structure of school. If we knew how to make friends in the real world, we wouldn't be asking this question. New homeschoolers wouldn't worry about their children having playmates. This tells me that we, as a society, have no idea whatsoever how to make a friend on our own. We depend on the structures of work and school so much, that many of us haven't learned how to go out in the world and create friendships.

So I wonder about the social structures of school. If being in school is such a great way to make friends, then why are we so scared to leave it? It's a social system that creates dependency.

Here's a secret that resourceful homeschooling know: We have everything we need in us to make friends. So do our children. And the world is a wonderful, inviting place to make wonderful friends and meet interesting people everyday.

The first step in deschooling is to learn this truth as an adult. Then, by our own understanding, we can teach it to our kids.

Making Our Own Communities

In some neighborhoods, the local homeschooling groups are highly visible. Everyone knows about them, and new homeschoolers find them without much effort because even non-homeschoolers know about the group. Schoolers go one place, homeschoolers go to another. There are practically arrows leading you to where you are supposed to go.

In most communities, however, homeschoolers are not given this roadmap. Just like everything else, new homeschoolers are given the unspoken challenge to figure it out for themselves. Most local homeschooling groups are quiet, don't advertise, and require quite a bit of effort to be found. Sometimes it's because there are many little pockets of homeschoolers that revolve around a program, or a religion, or method. Sometimes it's because the group has little money or resources to create an outreach program. But most of the time, it's simply because the group is not a formal program – it's simply a bunch of parents who have come together and created something that they needed.

In other words, as deschooling parents, we have to drop any expectation that someone is going to give us a pre-established place that we can select our friends from. We can no longer put the responsibility of making friends on someone else's shoulders. The only way we can do it is to get out in the world and get involved.

We are adults. It's time to take care of ourselves, and our families, and start building our community. Building relationships with the people in our world is our job. It's not the world's job to come to us. And it's not other homeschoolers' jobs to create a social network for us. It's our own social life, and we are the sole responsible owner of it.

In the process of creating that life, we will learn (if we don't already know), how to really make friends. We learn how to stop worrying about our children's social abilities. Real friendships, real communities, and real social lives don't develop overnight. It takes time, effort and experience to find where we belong. The first step to that journey is to get involved in the world. This is what experienced homeschoolers know, and why when we are asked "what about socialization," we chuckle. The world is our playground, why would socialization ever be an issue?

Do We Need Homeschooling Friends?

When I first started researching homeschooling, it took me a while to find our local homeschool groups. When I did find them, I was thrilled to have a life-line to other homeschoolers. Up until that point, I had only talked to homeschoolers online. In my real life, all my friends from the mom support groups were getting ready to send their kids to school.

Unfortunately, after visiting the local homeschooling groups, they ended up not working out for us. Either we didn't "click" with the group, or it wasn't a convenient time of day for us. I stayed in touch with them all, but didn't find immediate friends.

I was disappointed. I didn't have school to give me my social network, and I thought this was going to be the place to find my friends, and to find friends for my children.

What I thought was a disadvantage in the beginning turned out to be a blessing in disguise (for some reason, this happens to me a lot). It forced me to keep seeking friends in other places. The diligent person that I am, I didn't let not having a homeschool network stop me, and I kept looking anyway.

We started making friends at the library book club, at the local parks and recreation classes, at the bookstore, at restaurants we frequented, at the video game store. After some time, slowly, we created our social network around us. Most of our friends weren't homeschoolers. It was a strange realization that we could be happy, successful homeschoolers and our friends didn't have to all be homeschoolers, too.

When my oldest was seven, we started going on more field trips with one of our local groups. Through those trips, we started making more homeschooling friends. But by that time, I had learned that we didn't *have* to be friends with these people simply because they were homeschoolers. Of course we were friendly and enjoyed their company on the trips, but we didn't feel desperate for them to like us. We were free to create our own social network by the things we are interested in and with the people we felt the most comfortable with.

In essence, not being immediately wrapped up by the local homeschooling group gave us the opportunity to get lost in the social network of the world, and find our own friend-making path. It's not about going to a group and expecting someone, anyone, to like us. We are going to enjoy ourselves there, coming together with people who enjoy the same activities we do, and if we make friends, that's icing.

Being friends simply because we have the same kind of education was not enough to bring us close to people. Being friends because the kids were the same age, wasn't enough either. What brought us together to our friends, and kept us there, were compatible personalities and interests.

Instead of depending on an outside organization to provide a pre-made pool of possible friendships, we have the freedom go into the world and create our own pool with resourcefulness, perseverance, and chutzpa.

Joining Homeschooling Groups

It took a while to create the social circle we have today. There were times when I was tired of going out and meeting new people at every gathering. I did crave that comfortable place where I knew all my friends would be there, and we could visit in a relaxing way together. But I'm glad that I didn't latch on to anyone or any group simply because I craved that. Now, eight years after we moved into our neighborhood, we have a close group of friends who feel like family to us. And we still go out and meet new people all the time.

Not everyone will go through the same experience we had, of course. We all have different personalities; different levels of connectedness to our communities and different interests, few of us will have the same process on how we create our network. Our local homeschooling group touts over 100 families from diverse backgrounds. Many of those families are heavily involved in group activities, knowing all the people and making sure that there's always something going on. Others are casual participants, and their lives are intertwined with all the different people in the community outside of the homeschooling group.

Depending on what's available in your community, you may find integrating into the local homeschooling community to be straightforward, and a perfect match. But don't give up if that isn't the case. If you find yourself unable to find a welcoming group right away, keep looking around both in and out of the homeschooling community.

There is a lot of good opportunity in a homeschooling group. But they are just families like we are. So think of your local groups as one of the thousands of possibilities in your community. It's OK to take your time getting to know the group, and to find your own way to be involved in the homeschooling community.

The first step is to get "in the know" about your local area's groups. When you do your research, remember, you don't *have* to be involved in any one group. If it doesn't seem to fit right away, you have other options, including trying again in a few months when the kids are older or participating selectively in field trips and events. If the park day isn't your thing, see if they have a book club, or a mom's night out, where you can get to know a few individual families at a time, in a more focused environment.

Some of our best homeschooling friends were made outside of the larger group meetings. Having the shared experience of doing things together in a low-pressure activity such as a field-trip gave us a chance to get to know more people in a real-life non-park-day way. Now, when we go to park day, we enjoy it much more than we used to, because we have common experience.

You can find out about your local groups by doing an internet search, asking the local librarian if they know of any homeschoolers, and checking your state-wide website or newsletter. When you are visiting one group, ask what they suggest for new homeschoolers—is there a local hangout, are there homeschool-friendly businesses, are there any programs available in the community just for homeschoolers?

Another great way to get to feel comfortable in a new homeschooling group, or to get to know the community, is to volunteer. When you go to park day, or meet new homeschoolers, keep your ears open for opportunities to volunteer. When we are in a position of having something specific to do, it gives us a reason to talk to a lot of people without thinking about making friends or whether we get along. Volunteering also gives us a better idea of the general group dynamic in a more insider perspective.

Common Homeschooler Hangouts

Most homeschooling support groups have park days, which tends to be a new homeschooler's first contact with the local community. In our corner of Los Angeles, there are at least four park days within five miles of our house, each with their own group personality.

My friend Chrissy was literally saved by park day. When she pulled her 12 year old out of school, she had no idea where to turn, what to do. Then she found our local park day, and she and her daughter were hooked. She went from being unsure and alone to confident and involved within a few months. The change was so dramatic, I like to use her story at my information night meetings to show just how powerful support groups can be.

Another friend, Leslie, found her group of friends at park day too. She and her two small children were wary because there were so many new people there. After a few meetings, she happened to met a group of lovely people, and is now part of a sub-group that meets on a different day, just for the little ones.

While being around homeschoolers and getting involved in groups isn't an automatic set of friends, it does provide a great place to meet new people. Even in my own experience of not being incredibly involved in park day, I have met quite a number of friends there.

Another great homeschooler hang-out is the library. The library is a homeschooler's second home. The children's librarian can be the perfect matchmaker. Although not all homeschoolers who go to the library chat with the librarian, many do. So the librarians know who to talk to if you want to find out local information. Librarians often enjoy talking to homeschoolers too, because we come when it's not busy, we are genuinely interested in learning and reading, the parents usually accompany the children (even when they are teens) and we can volunteer when other kids and parents can't. Also, from what I hear from our local librarian, homeschoolers are just plain good people. Oh, she says they are smart and polite too. I won't argue with her on those points.

If you give your local children's librarian your contact information, she can keep an eye out for other homeschoolers that she meets. In our local area, I run an information night, and our librarian has been wonderful in getting the word out to parents about our meeting. She has also told me about other homeschoolers she meets, and when we are there at the same time, introduces us to each other.

For the technically inclined, online e-lists are a perfect place to find homeschooling camaraderie and support. In the recent years, the internet has become the de facto means of getting hooked up as a homeschooler. If you are in an area that doesn't have a lot of homeschoolers, or doesn't have a support group that you feel comfortable with, an online group can be a life-saver. Online support groups not only provide a place to chat, but pertinent legal information, local events, information on the different perspectives on home education, book suggestions and a place to brainstorm ideas. Can't figure out how to work math into your child's interest in Transformers? Ask your online group. Odds are, you'll get several great answers.

Non-Homeschooling Friends

"Life is partly what we make it, and partly what it is
made by the friends we choose."
  - Tennessee Williams

"True friendship isn't about being there when it's
convenient; it's about being there when it's not."
  - Author Unknown

In the beginning of our journey, I was so interested in homeschooling, it was all I talked about. I met a lot of parents who were willing to hash it out with me, discussing education, family life, ideas on how to get by. After a while, that topic kind of got old. Then I was left staring at my new friend, wondering what else we had in common. Being a homeschooling parent was enough of a common ground for the very beginning of a friendship. But to make lasting friendships, I had to find people who we could "hang" with, and talk with about many things, and enjoy doing things together. Just being a homeschooler brings us together as having something in common, just like school might be non-homeschoolers' common tie. However, what brings us into a deeper long-lasting friendship is something more. Instead, having similar life paths, and being comfortable with each other over the long term is more what keeps us friends.

Now, we have so many friends who aren't homeschoolers, I sometimes forget that we are. We are so focused on other interests, that homeschooling doesn't come up very often. And when it does, it's always an interesting conversation about different ways to look at education.

I have to admit though, that homeschooling friends are fun to have simply for the flexibility of being able to spend time together during school hours. When we want to play during the day, we pretty much are limited to our friends who don't go to school. That is, if they aren't busy doing their own stuff too.

Local neighborhoods can also be a great place to find friends. In our current culture, few of us know our neighbors. When we moved into our community, we didn't want to live the life of a hermit. We wanted to feel at least some camaraderie with our neighbors. In the beginning, our immediate neighbors to our right were the only ones with kids. When we met them, before we bought our house, they were out playing in the front yard, tossing a ball around. They waved "hi" to us, and asked us if we were thinking of buying the house. Having just one neighbor, with kids, who were willing to play in the front yard together as a family, was a strong selling point for us.

When we moved in, we played in the front yard too. I'd bring the baby out in her bouncer, and sit on the grass and read while the kids played. Or we'd kick a ball around. Gradually, more families moved in. Our new neighbors said that our playing outside and talking to them affected their decision to move in.

Now, our neighborhood has a wonderful group of kids and parents. We have ad-hoc front yard meetings several times a week. The kids take turns visiting at each others' houses. We pick up each other's kids from school, baby-sit, and go out to dinner together. We do talk about school quite a bit. Two of our neighbors are teachers, one works on a school staff. But it's not a huge topic (usually). By being out in the yard, connecting with our neighbors, we've attracted a certain kind of family to our neighborhood, and we've created a supportive group that's literally on our doorstep.

There are many other places to meet new people. In fact, anywhere we go, we have the potential to meet a new life-long friend. There are people everywhere. It's our responsibility to go out and put ourselves in the position to connect with people.

Ideas for Getting Hooked Up

- Joining Boy Scouts, Girl Scouts, 4H or other volunteer group
- Pursuing a hobby in a group situation, such as knitting circles, theater or sports
- Joining or starting a book club
- Going on field trips, either as a family or with a group
- Traveling

- Attending homeschooling conferences
- Taking a class at the local park and recreation, junior college, or arts center
- Attending museum programs and tours
- Organizing an event or program around an interest
- Inviting others to join you on outings
- Being in a receptive mood, so people will want to come up and talk while out and about

Getting the Kids Involved

Get your child's input in deciding which events to go to, and which friends to meet with. Some kids aren't ready to jump into the homeschooling social group. It's intimidating for some kids to go into a whole different world if they haven't had much experience with that in the past. If your child still has an attachment to his school friends, and does not want any new friends yet, that's OK. Or you may just hang out in your local community, and that's OK. If you know where the homeschoolers congregate, when child's ready, he can join them, one activity at a time.

Also keep in mind your child's social temperament. Just like we have learning styles, we all have social styles. What is "too much" and "not enough" friends and social activities will depend on our children's needs. There is not universal right amount of social interaction. And the kind of interaction we prefer, whether it be small groups, best-friends-forever, or large parties, is different for each us.

Making friends and interacting with the community and is a life-long experiment. We never stop learning how to make friends. Our children will make mistakes in this realm too, and so will we. But if we keep in mind their needs, and work to support them, rather than create their social world for them, we can't give them "too much" or "not enough". It's all a learning experience, and we make friends on that journey.

Keeping School Friends and Being "Weird"

Humans are at once fascinated and appalled by people who they
consider to be weird. This intense interest in things that are different is
perpetrated in school where standing out is very apparent. It's no
secret at how children torment each other in school about their hair or
looks or habits.

Depending on how old our kids are, and how attached they are to
school social rules; they may take issue with not being like their
schooled friends. Knowing other homeschoolers is not only
comforting, but it allows us to relax and not have to play the "rebel"
role all the time. For many kids, being comfortable around others is
easier when they have a lot of common ground. Going to homeschool
park days and events might ease the transition, and allow your child to
see that he's not the only one who is homeschooled.

There is a huge diversity of people here in Los Angeles. We have
friends of all different beliefs, cultures and political ideas. Even in our
own neighborhood, we have Catholics on one side, ex-Mormons on
the other, a Unitarian Universalist family two doors down, and then
there's us, an atheist-Buddhist-agnostic-whatever family. That's just
religion. Then we look at lifestyle – across a street a single mom, next
door a dual working family who spends every spare moment playing
sports, our other neighbor who is a stay at home mom who is going to
school herself, and two doors down, a teacher and a film editor who
aren't married, but it sure seems like they are. And then there was our
family, who our neighbors call the "normal" ones in the area. And
we're the homeschoolers!

We are fortunate to live in the area we do. Being so diverse, there
really is no such thing as "weird" here. Everyone lives is in their own
way. We've come to recognize that everyone's so different, if we took
offense to that, we'd be friendless very quickly. Weirdness is on a
sliding scale.

But in neighborhoods where the community is not so diverse, one
homeschooler can seem like a big red flashing light in the middle of a
panel of green.

If homeschoolers are so different compared to everyone else, is it inevitable that our children will be forever weird? In an essay I wrote for my alternative education blog, *Just Enough and Nothing More*, (justenough.wordpress.com), I look into the reasons why homeschoolers are accused of being weird, how those accusations are true, and why it doesn't matter:

Homeschoolers Are Indeed Weird

Homeschoolers, as individuals, are just as weird as public or private school families. As individuals, we all have our quirks. It just so happens, that homeschoolers aren't too troubled to hide those quirks, because there is a general feeling of accepting each other (while at the same time being confident in ourselves being who we are too.)

Homeschoolers are different than the rest of the population, purely because we've chosen a non-mainstream way to educate our kids. Instant weirdness. And, we are almost all opinionated, without much fear of how others might perceive us. Double weirdness.

Homeschooled kids are weird, just like the kids on the schoolyard. But instead of having that weirdness squelched out of them, homeschool kids are given less pressure to change their behavior in order to conform. They are often up front about how their opinions and interests are different than others. In other words, they don't have different opinions to prove a point. They don't have uncommon interests in order to stand out from the crowd. These interests are genuinely a representation of who they are.

Since these kids are all coming from their own unique perspective, just as any kid is, they are just as likely as school kids to judge each other's experiences as being "different". The younger the kids, the more likely they are to come out and say, "You don't do things the way I do." I don't have any fantasized expectations that all the homeschool kids I meet are going to be nice to my kids. I expect kids to be kids. They say things that aren't perfect. They make judgments.

But, so what if their friends (or even very un-friends) say they don't like something they are interested in? My children can say, "I'm not all that interested in what you think" and move on. In school that kind of statement is a test of "are you on my side or their side?" Homeschooling kids, even if they are living a totally different life than ours, aren't on anyone's side, they are on their own side.

That said, there are definitely "cliques" in our homeschooling group, both with the adults and the kids. The difference between the cliques in our homeschool group, and the ones in school, is that there is no exclusion based on that. People just get along with each other and tend to do the same kinds of things, so they hang out together. Although there might be differences of opinion of what is fun and good, there isn't exclusion or shunning based on this. (I realized that not all groups are like this. Homeschoolers are still people too, and are subject to the same social pressure as everyone else. I don't participate in groups laden with drama, homeschooling or otherwise.)

Homeschooling is not perfect, nothing is. But when it comes to learning how to get along with people in the world, educating kids in real world experience is better than kids being alone in their social battles. It's also better than kids having to live up to someone else's expectations of what is cool. And it's certainly better than kids having to face a 6-8 hour day of being in a closed-culture where so much attention is put on people who stand out.

Homeschooled kids are weird. I don't see why that's a problem. Doesn't school teach kids to deal with all kinds of people in all kinds of situations? If that's the case, what does it matter that a few homeschooled kids are weird? Since we all learned in school how to get along with each other, why should it matter that anyone is different?

The biggest critique of homeschooling is the "socialization" issue. If we use the world as our classroom, finding ways to socialize is not inherently a problem. But learning how to create your own circle of friends when it's not handed to us by the social structure of school is part of the deschooling adjustment process. Just like moving to a new city or new country, the easiest way to get to know people is to spend time in places where others share our common interests. That's what socializing really is about – learning where we belong.

Self-Discovery Questions:

- Where are your local support groups and park days? Who are the contact people?
- Do you have a statewide homeschooling organization? Do they have conferences or meetings? Where and when are they?
- Where are the local libraries, educational resource centers, park and recreation departments and bookstores?
- Is there a website, yahoo group or other online social networks for your state and/or educational perspective? How many do you belong to?
- What are some of the groups in your area, such as Girl/Boy Scouts and 4H?
- What is the general homeschooling atmosphere in your area? What is the history of homeschooling in your region and state?
- Who in your area can help you find resources, such as classes and volunteer opportunities?

Step 7: Become a Student of the World

"The only kind of learning which significantly influences behavior is self-discovered or self-appropriated learning – truth that has been assimilated in experience."
- *Carl Rogers*

"The glue that holds all relationships together – including the relationship between the leader and the led – is trust, and trust is based on integrity."
- *Brian Tracy*

"I never teach my pupils; I only attempt to provide the conditions in which they can learn."
- *Albert Einstein*

Who Is Doing the Learning Anyway, Parents or Kids?

Kids learn early on in school that the teachers expect a certain amount of role-playing. The teacher knows the information and is going to give it to the student. The student comes to class everyday, a passive receptor, and waits to find out what it is the teacher is going to impart on him that day. It's clear from the beginning – the teacher teaches. The student learns from the teacher. Then the students show the teacher that he has internalized what the teacher has taught.

It can be easy to fall into the "I'm the parent, do what I say because you're the kid" trap. But do these roles have to be put in such a black and white context? What would happen if we switched roles, and parents looked at themselves as students, and their children as their teachers?

Kids have so much to teach us. They can teach us patience, innocence, and how to think about things in a different way. They see the world with fresh, untainted viewpoints. They bring to the table a lot more than our society often gives them credit for.

Yet, how often are we able to fit this practically in our lives? How often can we appreciate the ways our children can help us grow?

We have been culturally trained that adults are supposed to be the ones in control, and act like it. That's what we're supposed to do right? Parents are especially motivated to put on this show. It's hard to imagine a responsible parent who doesn't at least seem like they have it figured out. But the truth is, none of us do. We are moving forward day-by-day, doing the best we can with what we have, just as our children are. There are still many things that we adults don't know. What we do know is that as we grow older, we have more responsibility and more doubts about whether we can keep it all together. We might know more facts or have more information in our heads than they do. Certainly we have more life experience than they do. But does that make us more right? Does it give us enough knowledge to know what every person needs to get along in his or her own life?

Whatever we know, is only marginally more than what our kids know, compared to everything there is to know in the world. And, what we so easily forget is that there are things that kids know better than we do, because we have grown out of many kinds of knowledge.

For example, children know how to love unconditionally better than most adults. Children also have a better grasp of how big the universe really is. And more importantly, they are more open to being a student of that world. At some point in so many of our lives, as we develop into responsible adults making a living for ourselves or our families, so many of us lose the interest, or ability, to keep looking for new things in the world around us. Besides the fact that we're supposed to have it all figured out, we have been taught through years of practice that learning new things is a tiring, emotional business. To rise above that and become a life long learner has to be a conscious choice. It's certainly not a practice that our educational system emphasizes.

Perhaps it's our human need for consistency and comfort, that once we find a world to live in that is straightforward and predictable, we don't want to ruin it by reaching out and bringing new things into that world. Maybe we are so distracted by the infinite to-do list of being an adult that we forget to play. And when we do play, we escape from the world instead of finding new ways to be a part of it.

Kids can teach us adults how to be students of the world. And, when we are students of the world, we can better teach our kids.

Putting Ourselves in Our Children's Shoes

It's easy to forget what it was like to see the world through the eyes of a child. Maybe we can remember what living with a teenage brain was like. (Who can forget pimples and fighting over curfews?) But for most of us it's really hard to remember much about our early childhood other than a few snippets here and there. And certainly, it's nearly impossible to remember what our view of the world was back then, before we developed abstract thinking, and before we accumulated all of the beliefs about the world that we have today.

Harder than anything else, is remembering the essence of being young, of discovery, of being so little compared to the rest of the world, and of wanting to be just like Mom and Dad who understand the world of grown-ups. Quite literally, children's brains are different than adult brains. And after we've developed out of our child brain, and into our logical, experienced, habitual thinking, it's challenging to remember how we viewed our world around us when we were children.

Modeling Life-Learning Behavior

If we look closely at ourselves now, we can probably find some residue of that childhood wonder. We can recognize residuals in our adult selves of our childhood drive to be like our parents. Children use their parents as models of how the world works, and often times we don't completely lose that habit as we grow into adults. Have you ever wondered if your mom would approve of something you're doing? I know that even now, having three children of my own, I still make some of my decisions partly in response to how my parents would have done it.

The most dominant message kids get about how to be an adult, and about what is important, come from parents. Younger children, especially, with their black and white inexperience with the world, look to their parents to know how to interpret the world around them. This is why what we do is far more important than what we tell them they should be doing.

When I was in high school, I remember being annoyed with our gym teacher because she never played the sports she asked us to play. She didn't do the exercises, and she didn't seem to have any interest whatsoever in the topic of P.E. She seemed to enjoy blowing her whistle, lining people up and marking our names on her list far more than she enjoyed sports or fitness.

As an adult, I can see why perhaps that teacher was unable to enjoy her job precisely because she wasn't able to play sports with us. She had to be the teacher, not the sports enthusiast. But as a kid, that information would not have made sense to me. It was impossible for any of us to get excited about something that we had no model for.

My son, when he was 8, joined a soccer team. He wasn't a very good player. In fact, he's kind of clumsy and a little oblivious. But he had a soccer coach that got into the game with the kids, kicked the ball with them and had a good balance of being "coach" and being "soccer enthusiast". My son fed off of him the desire to play soccer. No matter how well my son did, he had a fabulous experience. All the kids did. They laughed, were energetic and kept going on the field even when they were obviously going to lose. Their soccer vocabulary didn't have "loser" or "we're going to cream them!" or "cheater" or any of the other aggressive terms the other teams would use with each other. The soccer coach modeled a love of soccer, and friendly game play that was infectious. He hardly needed to "coach" at all.

Granted, I am a little biased about the awesomeness of our team. But I have to give the coach enthusiastic applause for getting those kids excited to play, no matter what level of ability they had.

Kids are intuitive. They know when we are asking them to do something that we don't find important. They may not tell us with so many words, but they know when we aren't being true to ourselves. In the end, kids will generally imitate the things we do, not the things we tell them to do.

Who Learning Belongs To

Whether our own educations were fraught with knuckle whacking and social trauma, or whether our memories of the school days are nothing but fun and frolic, we all hold on to a specific idea of what learning is supposed to be. For most of us, we were taught that learning happens in school, while everything else is... Well, something else. If it's assigned in school, it means something. If it's not, then it's not quite learning.

We are also taught that we don't possess a true sense of our own ability to learn. That's the teacher's job. The teacher is the one who is supposed to know the mechanics of learning, how our brains work, and what we are supposed to be able to retain when. The teachers are the ones who hold the key to the closet of important knowledge, and if what we want to learn is not in there, it's probably not important.

We are taught that it's not our job to seek out learning. It's our teacher, our boss, our shrink, our spouses, our parents, anybody but ourselves, who know what we are supposed to be learning. Children get this message all their lives, and as adults, we are far too willing to continue that legacy and keep the people around us informed of who they are, while we ourselves are trapped by other people's opinions of what's important.

At the same time, our culture impresses upon us the importance of individuality. The message we hear is to be unique and find our true selves, so long as we aren't "too" out of the norm. Rise above and do something better than everyone else, and do it bigger, brighter, and louder, within the context of what our culture deems as valuable. Take risks to be noticed, but if you fail by taking those risks, you'll be ridiculed by those who enjoy saying, "I told you so."

It's no wonder when it's time for us to teach our own children, it's a confusing mess. We get mixed messages from the world around us. Do we do what we want to do and potentially gain the scorn of those who think that what we've chosen is not worth it? Or do we do what we think we're supposed to do and try to make a place in this world by being the best at what everyone else already does?

And, as parents, are we supposed to let the kids be who they are, or do we guide them? Are we their friend or their dictator? Tell them what to do or let them fail and figure out how to succeed in their own way? How do we teach them to learn when we've got all these conflicting messages of what learning is supposed to be?

Regaining Our Sense of Life-Learning Enthusiasm

The only way to understand the process of learning in our children is to rediscover that sense of wonder in our own selves. We need to put ourselves in their place by learning something new, researching, asking questions, and being curious. Learning is thrilling. It's amazing. It makes us feel alive. As the saying goes, as soon as we stop learning, we start dying.

We can't teach that to our children unless we are living out that truth in our own lives.

Learning is not going out into the world to find more ways to continue being who we are right now. Learning is a challenge to keep changing. And when we, as adults, can find that willingness to continue growing and changing by learning new things that might change our point of view, change who we are, grow in front of the eyes of our family, then we've created a positive learning experience. We've gone out and done the very thing we want our children to do. Then, they see how invigorating it is to live a full and authentic life. They will be inspired to imitate the kind of joy we are discovering.

By having this experience ourselves, and by knowing what it feels like to be a student of the world forever, we can have confidence that our children can do this too. They see in us a positive role model for learning, and, how good it makes us feel to be learning. They can see the passion in our eyes when we talk about a new idea. They can see how once people become adults, we don't have to be stuck in recycled thoughts.

Being around people who are learning is invigorating. When our children are with us and we are in the midst of a positive learning experience, they may not agree with us that what we love is important, but they will feel the enthusiasm for life that we're giving off. That enthusiasm is contagious. And the more often we feel it, the more we want to feel it again.

The high of being a life-long learner is a drug that makes us better people. And when we are better people, more fulfilled people, more full people, we are happier, and can see what it's really like to learn, from our own, recent experience, and want nothing less from our children.

> *It's never too late to learn anything for which you have a potential*
> *- Leo Buscaglia*
> *Love*

Learning Is Always Available

One of the biggest misconceptions about learning is that there is a window of opportunity for academic subjects, and those children who get "behind", have lost that window.

This belief exists because school has created artificial windows of learning that can be missed.

Out of school, these windows don't exist. The truth is, in the real world, there is no such thing as "behind", and we can always learn something we missed along the way. Again, no matter what academic learning we missed as a child, the opportunity to learn it as an adult is always available.

If we are lifelong learners ourselves, we can see that nothing is so sacred that it can't be learned as an adult. By being an adult student of the world, we prove that to ourselves every day. When we know ourselves, in our own experience, that we can grow and continue to learn forever, we lose the fear that our children have to learn everything right now. Because if our children make it to adulthood having missed being taught something academic, they still have a life-long chance to learn it later if they need to.

Another marvelous discovery about being a life-learner, is that we do not have to learn everything. When we're stagnant, and unhappy, thinking about all the things we don't know, or that we missed, or that we'll never get to in our life, well, it's depressing. But if we are engaged in life, and doing those things that we really want to do, all the things we are missing don't really seem that big of a deal.

When we are doing what we love, and we know the things we need to know to be successful in our own lives, we don't need to know but a very small fraction of what there is to know.

Nobody can do everything. Nobody can learn everything. Nobody can be good at everything. Yet, our society expects that of children. We laud people who can answer random trivia questions like a computer.

That might even seem important to us as homeschoolers. Yet, when we have something we're passionate about, then, we see, that having a purpose makes all the stuff that we're not doing, that we're not good at, insignificant. Being a life-long learner in our own lives shows us what is really necessary to learn.

Learning to Be Patient

Many say that homeschooling requires a lot of patience. And I agree. But it's not the kind of patience we need to keep from yelling at our kids, and it's not the kind of patience we need to deal with a messy house. The kind of patience we need as homeschoolers is for the entire idea of how and when learning is supposed to happen. What we need to be able to do is to look at learning from a life perspective and see that there's no rush. The only rush that exists is our own expectations of what is supposed to happen.

While it's important to continue to try new things, go to new places, and see things from different point of views in order to grow, we don't have to do it all right now. Nor do we have to do it all at once. There is no rush in learning. Loving to learn means living life fully, not quickly. Loving to learn doesn't necessarily mean wanting to know everything there is to know in the world this very moment. In fact, that's overwhelming and a sure path to not actually learning anything significant.

Loving to learn, and being a student of the world, is an appreciation that there are things out there that are interesting. There's never a drought of more to explore. The abundance of things to learn isn't threatening, it doesn't challenge us to make sure we cover as much territory as possible; it is an endless pool of possibility that we can sip from. We don't have to drink every ounce of water in the pool to quench our thirst. When we see the world is a sea of opportunity, no matter what we choose to learn, it's going to be good.

Being happy with who we are, and what we are doing, and seeing our own selves as learners, gives us a healthy way to send the message to our kids just how important it is to be curious. This gives us reason to trust that that all they need is a passion for life. Keeping that insatiable need to learn and to grow is the goal. What they learn, the scope of what they know, will naturally grow and mature. Where they will go, it's impossible to say. But they will go somewhere, so long as they have the perspective that life is a never-ending growth process.

The learning we need is attracted to us like magnets. When we continue to learn as adults, we can see that in our own lives. When the student is ready, the teacher will appear. But we can only believe it if we are in the midst of it ourselves. Then we understand better what it is we're asking of our kids when we educate them at home.

The Benefit of Distracting Ourselves from Our Children's Process

I don't know about you, but when I start something new and interesting, I put 110% of myself into that new thing. It was no different for homeschooling. I was gung ho, ready for action. I was super-hero homeschool mom, and by gosh I was gonna do this thing right!

The poor kids; they were my little guinea pigs. I scrutinized them, studied them, and tried my hardest to do exactly what would be the best thing for them. This was all theoretically for them, so I wanted to make sure they were in every possible class, learning everything they could learn. Assessing all their minute movements in learning.

Well, it may seem like I was focusing on the kids, but what I was doing going through my own process and using my kids as the central focal point. Really, all the scrutiny and hyper-planning was all about me and my discovery.

It was indeed an important process to go through for me, and part of my deschooling. I needed to know as much about my kids as I could in order to be confident that I could offer those things that matched who they were. But once I had that figured out, continued pressure on them to learn, and give me more input made us all frustrated, because they knew it wasn't about them anymore, it was about me and my fears.

Because I was working so hard, I expected the kids should have been working hard too. It frustrated me when they weren't as enthusiastic about my exciting projects as I was. My approach bugged them as well because I was breathing down their necks every minute, and calling attention to things that made them self-conscious of whether they were living up to my desires.

Then, something funny happened. My husband got me involved in his Everquest guild. (Everquest is an online game that was popular in the late 90's, early 00's) I only played an hour or two a night, but I spent a lot of time thinking about it, and planning for it. I was also teaching fitness classes, and then I got involved in our state-wide homeschool group. Somehow, all at once, I got busy with my own interests and growth.

Now, being busy comes in many different forms. The kind of busy I was, came from a place inside where I was following my passions. I wasn't busy cleaning, cooking and doing errands. I looked forward to all the things I had on my list to do. And being with my kids was one of those things I enjoyed on my list. But because I was focused on my own pursuits too, I didn't have time to obsess about the kids. I had just enough time to do what needed to be done with them, such as cuddling, reading, classes, field trips, and those kinds of things. But I didn't have time to hover over them or to micromanage them.

Talking with my friends is one of my passions. I can't tell you how much the kids have learned because mommy was distracted talking. One time, when I was talking to my neighbor longer than I planned, the kids found a worm in the dirt. Another time, I met a mom unexpectedly in a bookstore, and the kids ended up pouring over a book on mummies. These lessons I learned was that my children don't need me to fill their time every second of the day. They are capable of finding things to do without my consistent "help". While I'm busy doing the things I love, they are busy learning the things they need to learn. And when we come together, we have a lot to talk about. And being together is relaxed, not stressed.

Being a student of the world distracts us just enough from our kids' process that it allows them to own it. And our role then becomes less of a "do this, do that" role, and more of a "I'm curious about you and who you want to be." "How can I help?" "How can I join you?"

We don't ever want to get so distracted into our own world that we ignore our children, or are apathetic towards them. That's an escape, not an inclusive sharing of our passions. As parents, there is a balance to be found between taking care of ourselves and being there for our children. If we love ourselves, and treat ourselves with respect, we'll do the same for our kids. We won't ignore them.

Generally speaking, we treat other people as a reflection of how we feel about ourselves. If we are confident in our own abilities to learn, and to grow, we'll be confident that other people can too. If we cling to our passions as a way to prove something, then we'll be constantly looking at our kids to prove themselves to us. If we think we are unable to teach our kids what really needs to be learned when the time comes, then we will distrust their ability to learn it. If you want to know how you feel about your own learning, look at how you see your children's ability.

Creating a solid self, as a parent, keeps us from having to use our children to provide that self for us. Hovering over our children so that they will do well, and keep "on track", is a way to make ourselves feel better about the future, as if to say that, if we can't be perfect, maybe our kids can. But there is no perfect. Feeding our own soul with nourishing experience paves the way to nourishing our children's souls as well.

When, Ellie, a fellow homeschooler, wrote to our support group e-list that her 2nd grader had an issue with not doing her homework, it didn't immediately stand out. Parents trying to recreate school in their homes get frustrated often, and the topic comes up quite a bit on our lists. Usually, parents are at their wit's end because they can't figure out how to make things work, and weren't willing to actually change anything they were doing.

But this story was different. Ellie told us of how she became so frustrated with her daughter that she took the novel approach of asking her 8-year-old what she wanted. Ellie didn't really expect a response, but her daughter surprised her, and told her, "I like the subjects, but I don't like the way we're learning it. It's boring this way."

Ellie, not knowing what to do next, went on a search to find a better way to teach her daughter the subjects she wanted to learn. She told us how she kept coming back to unschooling. Then, she would get scared that it wasn't "real" learning, and then go back to school at home, which ended up being a battle. Her daughter was telling her how she wanted to learn, but Ellie was afraid to listen. After reading more and doing more research online, Ellie decided to give unschooling a try and see what would happen.

She said that she would teach her daughter in the same way she taught her before they started school. In a way, she went back to how things worked before she was "homeschooling" her daughter, teacher her about math and language in the same way she taught her how to walk and talk.

Ellie also put herself in her daughter's shoes, and imagined what it would be like to be forced to learn in a way that didn't work for her. In the "real world", we have a choice. Shouldn't we be teaching our children how to learn in the real world, where people aren't forced to do things they don't want to do?

Ellie's husband told her that he didn't have a choice in his job. She was frank with him and told him that when he went to interview for the job he learned what he would be doing, what his hours would be, and the expectations of him. He figured out how long he would have to drive, if the salary was enough for them to live on, if the insurance was good, and if the dress code was acceptable for him. When he accepted the job he made his own decision that he was agreeing to all the benefits and responsibilities of the job. He didn't have to agree to the terms. And nobody was telling him that if he didn't take that job, he'd go to jail.

So, instead of forcing her child to do her work, Ellie made the effort to learn to negotiate with her so they could both be happy. She changed her methods from expecting the right answer from her daughter, to exploring topics with her, as a companion.

Even so, even after two years of this kind of approach, her daughter, who had been in school for only one year, still expected to be told whether her answer was right and to gain Ellie's approval. Ellie said that a lot had to do with her own mistakes and how she had framed her relationship with her daughter as a homeschooling mom. They were working on redefining what they expected from each other. That change went both directions, and it's something they are still working on today. It may even be a life-long effort as she and her daughter both continue to deschool themselves, and find each other.

Understand What Our Kids Are Going Through

I was talking to our local librarian one day, expressing my love of young adult fiction. She responded saying that the books were dark, and depressing. And that it was changing the way kids looked at the world. Her conclusion was that adults don't understand how kids think, and when they write for them, they are writing for themselves.

Now, I'm not 100% convinced this is true. I mean, when I was a teen, I read a ton of Steven King and disturbing science fiction that I wouldn't go near now that I'm a child-rearing adult. There's something about the macabre and dark that appeals to the teen mind.

But she is right that adults have a hard time remembering what it's like to be a kid. Sure, we have memories of what we did, and we remember the bad decisions we might have made. But can we remember and appreciate the thought processes that brought us to those decisions? Can we remember what it was like not to know? To be in a position where we were still discovering the world?

To be able to meet our children where they are at, and help them develop at their own pace and style, it's important to rediscover our inner child. In Buddhism, it's called "the beginner's mind." When we see things with a beginner's mind, we look at what we've always been doing as if it were the first time. Not only does it give us a true sense of why our children make the decisions they do, it also improves our ability to see beyond our own view of reality.

As adults, we've established our patterns. The habits we've accumulated over the years have worked in one way or another. Why then should we bother moving out of those habits, and instead of keeping our lives right where they are now? It's scary to try something new; it might change us. And most of us are comfortable where we are, even if we may not be completely happy with where we are.

But for the sake of our children, and for our own sakes, we need to honestly face the reality of what our old habits create for us, and admit when we need to make change in our own way of seeing the world. It might seem advantageous to stay where we're at, but to be truthful, change is invigorating. It's scary, and sometimes hurtful. But most of the time, change brings positive movement into our lives. When we are stuck, or scared, or don't know why we are so unfocused, starting up something new is exactly what we need to get into a new realm of understanding, love, and meaning.

Being learners brings us to a place where we can appreciate and empathize with what our children are going through. They aren't having the exact same experience we are, and we can't expect them to: we're adults, they're children/teens. Not to mention, we're entirely different people with different personalities and goals. However, we are experiencing the same kind of newness. We are going through the growing pains of change together.

We can become a kid again. We can join our own kids, traveling the world together, knowing that this tour is a different experience for each person. Since we each get different things out of our travels, we can only benefit from the variety, by working together and learning from each other.

Getting Rid of Our Own Baggage

Julie's Story: *"It's hardest with the oldest because we are having to change our own ideas of what school and education mean in a homeschool environment. I realized that much more than my son needing to change, I needed to change. That's not to say he didn't have a responsibility back to me as a partner in this educational journey, just that how I saw our relationship in this journey was different than a classroom teacher-pupil relationship."*

"We can't give what we don't have." In other words, if we want homeschooling to work, we, as parents, have to get our own lives in order.

Most homeschoolers carry some baggage from their own life experiences. We pick certain methods as a way to deal with our own emotional uneasiness. If we were told that we weren't disciplined enough, we might have a system that's full of have-tos and lists, to prove "them" wrong. If we were bad at math, we might work hard to make sure that we have the perfect math system. If we were an A student, always expected to be the perfect child in school, we might look for a way to show that we still are.

Worse still, we put that baggage onto our kids. We might worry they will be slackers like we were, or we push them to have the same performance that we expected ourselves to have as children, but never did. From my experience, the things we worry about our kids and their education stem from some unresolved issue we have in our own lives.

Although this might sound like pop-psychology mumbo jumbo, we can't ignore it. We need to deal with our own educational baggage so we don't run the risk of giving it to our children to bear on their shoulders.

To do that, we can recreate a new, healthy relationship with our own learning. We can build a relationship where we trust ourselves as being capable, despite having weaknesses. We need to know what it's like to look at ourselves and not stress over whether we're good enough. We have to remember what it was like before we were caught up in our own web of trying to live up to an external ideal of a perfect spouse, parent, or person.

When we figure out who we are as learners, and we accept ourselves as we are, we are less likely to hand down our issues to our kids, which will allow them to have a healthy relationship with learning.

How we struggle with our kids is more a reflection of our own inner demons than a reflection of our teaching style. Being a learner in the world, whether it be an inner journey, or an outer one, brings us to a more balanced place in our hearts. If we struggle with our loved ones, odds are we need to clean our own mess, somewhere, inside our psyche.

> *"And as we let our light shine, we unconsciously give other people permission to do the same. As we are liberated from our fear, our presence automatically liberates others."*
> - *Marianne Williamson*

Becoming a student of the world has so many benefits for our homeschooling journey. It gives us a wider perspective of what learning is for, helps us understand our children and inspires our children to want to be life-long learners too. But it is also an enjoyable way to live. In the end, that's what it's all about, enjoying our lives together.

Self-Discovery Questions

- What is your relationship with learning, now, as an adult? How do you obtain new information when you need it?
- What is your learning style? How about your spouse and children?
- Is there anything that you've wanted to learn but never dared? What's stopping you from learning it now? What can you do to provide a good role model for your children on how to learn new things, even if they are hard or scary?
- Are you a micromanager? Or an under-manager? Think about how you manage your household and life, and how it effects your children's learning process. What do you prefer – a teacher who is very hands-on, or one that lets you learn at your own pace? What about your children? What do they prefer?
- What is out in the world that you've always wanted to see or do? What can you share with your children because you love it? What activities or hobbies give you the positive energy that your kids can inherit?

Step 8: Don't Keep Records, Keep a Journal

Facing the Accountability Goblins

Some states require that homeschoolers keep records of what they have accomplished. But none of the states require detailed records of every little thing that the kids are doing. They just want to see a snapshot.

That's what the state wants. But what good does this record do for us, as a deschooling family?

It may seem like a set of records will make us feel better about what we're doing and help us feel like we're accomplishing something. But during the deschooling process, keeping records often has the opposite effect – it keeps us tied into what we are "supposed" to be doing and takes our focus away from our family goals. Keeping records can make us scared that we aren't doing enough.

Record keeping is an invention of school process. Before schools, record keeping was only important when we needed to keep track of our finances or our business. People didn't keep track of what kids learned. When schools suddenly had thousands of kids to keep track of, records were necessary to keep things from becoming a confusing mess. It is also used to keep the parents informed about what was happening in school everyday. (Although, some would argue that it doesn't do a very good job of that either.)

Now, in the age of technology, where record keeping is so easy to do, we want to know down to the minute quantum detail what's going on. In an educational setting, that translates into lots of numbers and lists.

When we are living life and learning, we don't need to keep records. Do we have to keep records of everything we did when we visit relatives and go on vacation? Do we have to keep records when we are planting a garden? Do we have to keep records when we are fixing up a car? We don't need to keep records when we are learning either. Record keeping is for cows and coins. Not children.

So, throw those records out the window (except for the bare minimum that the state wants you to keep). And instead, buy a blank book and a video camera, and keep a journal.

A journal is for the family. Nobody is going to see it but the people in the family (unless, of course, you want to publish it several years from now and make big bucks in the homeschool market). The purpose of the journal isn't to document for others that what we are doing is legitimate. A journal is to bring all the things that we love about our lives, and what we've learned about our world, into one place. Our journal is a snapshot into who we are as a family.

Making a journal should be fun. It's fun because it's a time to re-live the things we're doing, sharing them once again with our family, and reinforcing memories.

A journal isn't necessary to deschool. But if is at all difficult to let go of the world of school and shoulds, a journal gives you a place to say the things you need to say. It can provide an anchor to peruse on those cold nights of waking up in a sweat feeling like we didn't do enough math instruction. A full journal reminds us to bring our focus back to our family and educational goals. A journal is also great fun to look back at, like looking at a photo album.

How Much Is Enough?

In our family, we live a life of organized chaos. Organized chaos is the idea that we keep just enough organization to make it workable, but not so much organization that it creates diminishing returns. After a certain point, cleaning and keeping track of things takes time away from actually doing things that are important. It also takes mental energy that can be spent on living life and puts it towards stressing, which in my opinion, isn't a very good way to spend my time.

We have made a pact in our house (well, hubby and I, anyway), that if something causes more stress than it makes things easier, something's got to change.

For a while, I was adamant about getting the house organized. The bookshelves were pristine, everything was in a basket or plastic bin, all the dolls were stored in bags with their own clothes and accessories, games were neatly stacked in the closet.

It was beautiful. It was also a lot of work and energy to keep it that way. I was constantly nagging the kids and my husband to put things back the way they found them. I used a lot of my own energy either snapping at the kids to keep things neat, or doing it myself. I found myself so obsessed with keeping things clean and neat, that my beautiful organization system was taking me away from enjoying my children.

There had to be a better way. I had to find a way to keep my desire for a certain amount of clean, while significantly reducing the amount of stress that was created with keeping the house the way I wanted it. I eventually swallowed my fear of not having a clean house, and looked at the diminishing returns of what my obsession with clean was doing to my relationship to my kids. We agreed on three or four places in the house that were to be kept clean so that we all have a shared place to work and play, and I let go of the rest.

I let the kids throw books on the bookshelves, let them stack games haphazardly or in the wrong place, and let them mix Polly Pockets with Mr. Potato Head pieces. All this has created chaos. But those three or four spots –the dining room, living room table and floor, and my desk – are kept clear of stuff that isn't being actively used. We created the minimum necessary to have a place to work without creating stress.

Although this is hard for my natural desire to be organized and tidy, it has made my life a whole lot easier, letting go of the things that don't absolutely have to be done, and letting the house, and the stuff in the house, settle naturally. Of course, once in a while I just *have* to clean something (usually as a way to procrastinate or reclaim control). But it's not an everyday stress of making sure the whole house stays pristine. I have found that place of "just enough" – organized chaos.

This is what a journal is for – to do just enough, but no so much that we have diminishing returns. It's just enough to keep track of the things that have been happening, but not so much that we are stressing over what we are writing down. Being free to pick the best things, and to write about them with love and a personal perspective, is a lot less stressful than having to keep track of every single detail of what the kids are doing.

Plus, during deschooling, many of the things that the kids do aren't going to be measurable by a test, grades, or records. You know they are learning, but keeping records won't reflect that precisely. (The one exception is if the state requires homeschoolers to keep these records, then you may have to translate some of what you are doing into education-ese. For information on reporting appropriately to your state, consult your local or statewide homeschooling organization.)

The question really boils down to this: where do we want to spend our precious life energy? Do we want to spend it making sure the kids do things that can be put in a record book? Or would we rather spend it living life, and then re-living it again in a journal?

Focus on the memories you are making. If you find that you let the journal fall to the wayside, and don't make entries for a while, don't beat yourself up! In fact, you deserve congratulations. Not having time to journal means you are busy enjoying your life. You're getting away from the school idea that a child's life has to be completely documented and organized in order to assure that they are growing up.

We know our kids are learning without records, and we know we're doing our jobs well by looking at our children. If school did not exist, homeschoolers would have no need to create records. The reason why we feel that need is because that's what schools do.

There will probably be times when you feel like you're not doing enough and you might question this whole process. That's normal and that's when having a journal is so important. If, in your journal, you feel like documenting every single thing you did, and how it pertains to learning, do it. But do it for you and for your family. Do it because it makes you feel good to do it. Not to prove to anyone that you're doing what you should be. Use the journal to practice using your own judgment and educational goals to gauge your progress.

Ideas for Using a Journal

Revisit the family and educational goals you wrote back in step 5. Put those on the first page of your journal. If they change along the way, edit them or write a new entry. Then, when you feel like you aren't doing enough, go back to those goals that you wrote, with your family, and journal about whether you think you're living up to your own goals. And then reassess, in your journal, talking to yourself, what you need to adjust to better achieve those goals, or whether your goals are not really what you wanted in the first place.

List three things you love and appreciate about your kids. Then list three things they learned without your help. Then, continue to write whatever else you feel that day.

Make a graph of your deschooling process. Colleen Paeff wrote this graph in her journal, and then posted it on her blog at *The New Unschooler,* http://thenewunschooler.blogspot.com.

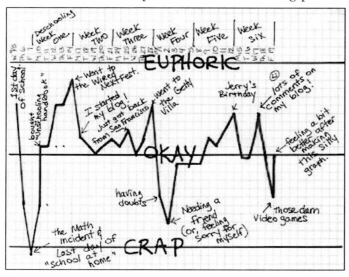

Instead of a journal, make a scrapbook. Some families make a scrapbook for each grade or year, as their memory book, journaling important information next to the pictures.

Blog your homeschooling journey. Remember, records take our focus away from the kids and towards an outside way of measuring whether we are doing enough. Right now, the most important thing is to be with the kids, without judging or measuring them. Get a feel for what it's like. And ask yourself, how much does having records actually change the way I teach, the way we live, and how the kids feel about their learning?

Years from now, when we look back at our time with our children at home, having a journal to remember with will be a treasure. Records, just like all of our school records, end up filed or thrown away like a calendar. It's not interesting to see what was on our schedule. It's interesting to remember what we had a great time doing.

Relatives Who Want to Check Up on the Kids

The State isn't the only place where we have pressure to keep records of what our kids are doing. Our relatives might want to see what our kids are up to too. Are we doing enough? Do we know what we are doing? Where's the proof? Here we have a great opportunity to create a journal and share it with our relatives. It keeps them up to date and keeps them happy that we're doing a great job with our children – because we care enough to share with them what we are doing.

Sharing our children's successes gives grandma and grandpa something they can be proud of when they talk about their grandchildren with their friends. A journal or regular updates on what we are doing gives them that wonderful keepsake. And might be a great way to disarm those "are the kids doing enough?" questions.

So the question is what to send the relatives? In this case, a simple rundown of what's going on might be the easiest thing to do. Or maybe they would prefer to have some samples of the kids' masterpieces, a letter listing their achievements, or perhaps pictures. A conversation on the phone might be enough. Or maybe they would prefer having one-on-one time with the grandchildren.

I prefer incorporating the family into our lives as much as possible as a way to appease their worries. I invite them to recitals, ask if they would help teach the kids something they know, or ask them to come with us on field trips. For the family that is not immediately available, I have a blog with pictures and essays about the things we are doing. I try to include the most interesting things we do, and phrase it like it's our normal everyday life to do interesting stuff like that *all the time*.

I started my blog for my family. But it has turned into my own journal. It's a keepsake of what we are up to, spanning back to about a year before my third child was born. I love going back and reading the archives. They are full of happy memories.

I also have a memory box for the kids, where I keep anything I think I might want to look at later (or that the kids would like to look at). I have so much stuff in that box and on my blog, that if I ever needed to make records of what the kids have done, I could do it with a couple hours of going through all of our stuff.

Both my blog and my memory box are fun to keep up. I don't stress over it, or consider it a chore. These things are fun projects.

What If the Kids Go to School?

Some families like to keep records in case their kids go to school at some point later.

Regulations vary from state to state, even district to district. It's important to know what your state public schools do with incoming homeschoolers.

Generally speaking, kids younger than high school don't need records of their schoolwork. New entry students in Grades 9 and younger are placed with their same-aged peers.

If your child is going into high school, records might make a difference in which classes they are placed. But it's also likely that those records won't make a difference at all. In our district, high school students who start after 9th grade don't get credit for any work or grades they bring in unless they were taken through an accredited school that the public district recognizes. And even then, some parents have had some trouble with the credit transfers. On the other hand, I have talked to parents in other districts that let the high schoolers test into AP or other advanced classes.

If you are considering homeschooling a high schooler, contact your local schools well in advance to find out what their process is.

In most cases, keeping meticulous records won't make a difference anyway. The most a school wants are grades and a few samples. Nobody will want to know the every day details of which pages your child completes, or which day he learned how to do fractions. That information is not important in a legal or practical sense. Before you decide to cover the what-ifs with meticulous record-keeping, do meticulous research on what kind of information is really needed. Instead of doing the daily work of keeping detailed records "just in case", do the work to learn for yourself what kind of information is necessary to keep for your state or you child's particular circumstance.

What about Records for College?

Every college has different requirements for homeschoolers and other alternative education students. So, keeping general records of a teen's classes, work, volunteering, self-taught education, and sample of his work, is a good idea. Some colleges and universities don't want any of that, but some will.

The way you keep records of all of this is the same way you would keep records for a resume when you apply for a job. As long as it's true, you don't have to keep "proof" that the child did it. If they volunteered for a pet rescue program, you don't have to keep the pictures of him holding a dog as proof. Just record the dates he did it, the name of the organization, and any letters of recommendation he might have received. If your teen took a class at the local community college, keep record of the semester he took it, the name of the college and the grade he received.

As soon as you know which colleges your child is considering applying to, find out what their requirements for alternative students are. Give yourself plenty of time. And keep an eye on any changes that occur, as it gets closer to application time.

And don't forget that many colleges allow students to apply as a sophomore or junior. Most kids are trying to get into college at the freshman level. So if your teen can get enough units at his local community college to apply as a sophomore or junior, he may not even need high school records at all. And he may even have a significantly higher chance of being accepted than all the students trying to get in as a freshman.

Self-Discovery Questions

- In thirty years, what would you like to have to look back on during this time? What kind of memories would you like to store?
- What are the minimum requirements of your state for keeping records? How do other parents in your state or region abide by the state's requirements without getting burned out? Even if you aren't an unschooler, ask an unschooler or two in your state how they abide by your state's records laws.
- If your state doesn't have record keeping laws, ask yourself when you would actually need to use records. Again, ask other homeschoolers when they've used records.
- Don't like keeping journals, or don't feel like you could remember to do it? Think about blogging, scrapbooking or keeping a memory box. What kind of memory storage are you the most comfortable with?

Step 9: Evolve Gently Into a New Homeschooling Life

"If you always think the way you always thought,
you'll always get what you always got."
- Gerald Haman

"No single step in the pursuit of enlightenment should
ever be considered sacred."
- Carl Sagan

One Thing at a Time

Sometimes, making a big change requires drastic measures. But most of the time, making permanent life changes starts with small, simple steps, and focusing on one change at a time.

It can be overwhelming to try to do it all at once. Human nature is to keep things just as they have always been. We are more likely to be successful if we focus our energy on making one change at a time.

Learning how to homeschool is kind of like learning how to eat healthy. Many of us struggle with our diet and weight. Diet books abound telling us how we can kick-start our metabolism, or lose 10 pounds in a week. Despite the fact that that these quick fixes don't work in the long run, the books fly off the shelves. We keep trying to jump into some extreme program with all the good intentions in the world, but it doesn't stick.

These kinds of diets don't stick because they aren't lifestyle changes. Rarely does fasting or taking out all carbohydrates or fat for a given time change our diets in the long run. The kinds of changes that change our lives for the better are things that we can permanently add to our lives. Starvation-based diets (which is pretty much any diet that requires very low calorie count) don't bring around change. They make us feel like we are in control, but they don't bring long-term life changes.

If we are committed to finding solutions and making lasting, positive life changes, small focused efforts can lead us there.

Deschooling is a lifestyle change. It's a change we make for the long haul. It is not a diet. We shouldn't be depriving ourselves in order to get ahead. And it's not a time for gluttony. (Well, OK, maybe a little, especially if we've been depriving ourselves from healthy brain food for so long.) It's a time to walk away from the cafeteria that feeds everyone the same food without explaining to us why, and without letting us question whether the food we are being served is healthy or even food at all. It's time to learn on our own how to feed our brains.

Making life changes that stick comes from doing things a little at a time. This is the same advice nutritionists suggest to those who have a hard time identifying what is "feel good" body food, and what is actually "feel good now, but feel bad later" food. Start with one thing at a time.

Add little things here and there that will work you closer to a balanced education and toward the space where you feel more comfortable. Start off with identifying where you are struggling the most. Use your journal to help you pinpoint one thing that you'd like to work on.

Important Things First

Have you heard the expression "choose your battles"? What this expression means is, if we make everything into a battle, then when it comes time to deal with the really important things, they will get lost in all the noise. How can our kids know what is really important when we are making a big deal about everything?

We can make the most effective and lasting change by focusing on the most important things first, and letting everything else take care of itself for a while.

Relationships, for example, are one of the most important things. Before we can work together with anyone on our homeschooling approach, we have to have good relationships.

Family values are also high on the list. And some values are higher than others. Listening and understanding are also high.

But you might find that recurring morning battles might be the biggest issue, or mealtime frustration gets everyone on edge. Focus on the one thing that will make the biggest change, and let the other frustrations take a back burner. When you are faced with a non-essential problem, say to yourself, "I recognize that is important, but I will not deal with it right now. I'm focusing on the important things. I will come back to it later when the important things have been taken care of."

Of course, you don't want to ignore when someone is in danger. But the majority of the time, we can let things go while we are working on the most important things, and everything will be fine.

Video Games Struggle

For many families, television-viewing and computer games are a point of contention during deschooling. Kids who are finally free to direct their day often end up focusing a lot of time on TV and video games. It's a forbidden fruit, and very engaging. And it can be a struggle for mom and dad to know what to do about it. Fortunately, there are also several ways to incorporate video games in our deschooling lives in a way that makes everyone happy.

The first step is to identify the reasons video games are an issue. If we believe the media, playing video games is a vague practice that hovers between watching TV and doing drugs. And as parents, we are told by the experts to limit the amount of time our kids play video games. But when we are in it, watching our kids play hours upon hours of video games, what is it exactly that makes us uneasy about them? What is their true role in our children's lives?

Common Video Games Concerns

We're afraid of being a bad parent. Our society puts a lot of pressure on parents to limit their kids' screen time. If we allow them to play video games as long as they want, we're being permissive. However, if we put arbitrary time limits on computer games, our kids can become obsessed or angry, and we are then sacrificing our relationships with them. That's not being a good parent either. If we deal with video games from the perspective of whether or not we're being a "good parent", a solution is elusive

They aren't learning anything useful. Part of our cultural mythology is that video games are brainless escapist activities that don't teach us anything useful in the real world. Yet, why is it that so many engineers, scientists, graphic designers, computer programmers, and other incredibly mathematically talented people play video games?

They aren't doing anything else but play video games. This is probably the biggest worry of deschooling parents. Kids get lost in hours and hours of video game time to the exclusion of other things. (This can happen with other activities too.) We worry that if all they do is play video games, that something bad will happen. Either they will turn into social misfits, or they won't be well rounded. Although I ask you to think about exactly what will happen if a kid plays video games to the exclusion to everything else. Why are they doing this and nothing else? Are video games really the issue here?

Their brains aren't developing normally. One worry is that kinds will not develop normally if they play video games. If we worry about this, we need to define "normal" and ask where that definition comes from. Do we have any empirical evidence of this happening? If so, is playing video games all day the reason it's happening, or is it the symptom of another issue?

They are getting behind in other things. This worry comes from still being entrenched in school-think. Outside of school there is no "behind". For parents whose children are in school, and their success in school is an important family value, getting behind is a real concern. However, in life, how can we get "behind"?

They are being exposed to violence and sex. Depending on a child's age, this can be a legitimate concern. Fortunately, not all games contain questionable material.

They act out or withdraw. If a child is acting out more than normal or withdrawing into video game playing, it might be a way to escape difficult emotions or life stresses. Unilaterally blaming video game playing isn't getting to the bottom of the issue. Often times, there is much more going on than simply playing too many video games.

They are addicted. Video game addiction is a real world issue. As with most addictions that do not involve physical dependency, the addiction tool is not at fault. There's something deeper going on that manifests itself in addictive behavior. In the case of addiction, dealing with the core issue will be more effective than trying to manage the symptom on the surface.

Concerns about video games vary. The most common way to deal with video game issues is to restrict or eliminate video game playing. Although this approach might work on the surface, it can create other problems in its place, such as power struggles, broken relationships, arguments, whining, complaining, "silent treatments," and mistrust. What putting limits on video games boils down to, is a declaration by the parent that they are in control, and that what the child wants isn't important. Parents do this with the assumption that they know what's best for their child. But I will argue that most parents do not know what is best for their child when they limit video games.

Most parents today did not grow up with video games. In addition, most parents do not play video games, or have any interest in the kinds of video games that today's kid plays. Because most parents do not have the personal experience of what it is like to play video games and how the brain processes video games on a personal level, there is no way that parents can know what's best for their children in this regard.

Putting limits on kids might work on the surface, but it's not dealing with the bigger issues of why kids play so many video games. Kids play a lot of video games for a reason.

I can say all of this, because I was one of the first generation of kids to grow up as a video gamer. My parents brought an Intellivision (the 1979 equivalent to the Wii), into our house when I was eight. I fell in love with it, and spent hours upon hours playing it.

Since then, playing video games on Nintendo, Gamecube, PlayStation, Gameboy, Wii, PC's and Macintosh have been a part of my life. There were times the games took over, much like a sports fan might be fanatical about a specific team. There were times that I played a little less because of other interests. But video games have *always* been part of my life.

When I was in college, I would have video game parties with my friends, where we would sneak into the computer lab where we worked, and spend all night playing Spaceward Ho!, a space exploration game with lots of interstellar battles. When I was in grad school, I would run down four flights of stairs from my office to the 3rd floor computer lab in between classes to play games. When my husband and I were dating, we would go to a video arcade, or stay home and play our computers together. When my children were babies, I nursed them while playing Everquest, and online multiplayer role playing game.

I *am* a gamer. I grew up a gamer. So, the perspective I have when my kids play video games is one of experience. Video games are just like any other hobby. They are not a problem in and of themselves. Video games are only a problem if we can't understand why our children play, and treat it like a forbidden fruit.

From my experience as a gamer, raising kids who like to play video games, here are some ideas on how to manage video game playing without using an iron fist. These approaches will help you maintain balance, maintain your relationships, and your kids will have the freedom to enjoy their hobby in a healthy, satisfying way.

Keep a varied schedule. Having a lot of fun, interesting activities is a positive life change, which solves many video game struggles. But the reason to take this kind of lifestyle approach is bigger than just trying to manage video games. Having a fun and varied life brings us all an awareness of what it's like to be active and engaged in the world.

That's the main benefit, while managing video game play is a natural side effect of this. Lead a happy life, with lots of good things, and you can let the kids play as many video games as they want, because they won't have the opportunity to play games to the exclusion of everything else.

Ask for game time of your own. A great way to connect with someone who is very involved in something is to get involved with that activity. We don't have to get as involved as our kids are, and we don't have to play all the time, but having a general experience with it can help connect by having a common experience, and something to talk about together. Also, if we sit down and play our own games, we need the computer, which creates a natural need for cooperative time management.

Negotiate a family rhythm. If one of the problems with video games (or anything else) is that once they go on, nothing else gets done, and the kids "zone out", one solution is to negotiate a list of things that have to get done before they can start video games. There are three major keys to this approach: First, make sure that the things that need to be done have a clear reason for being accomplished (for example, meeting family goals). Secondly, make sure that everyone in the family is adhering to the same restrictions so that the kids don't feel like they are victims. In other words, live what you believe and have integrity. If you enjoy crafting or some other hobby, put that off until everyone is done with their work. Lastly, give the kids as much control as possible. If you can, make the daily chores or have-tos as broad as possible so that the kids can create their own day. With this approach, once everything we feel is important is done, the kids can play unlimited video games and we won't feel guilty. In addition, the kids will feel like they get to do what they enjoy.

Have a pocket of activities ready. If your kids tend to get snappy, or agitated while playing video games, having some activities ready to do for a "break", gives us a way to help kids manage their own video game time. Doing something outside, in my opinion, is one of the best ways of taking a break. Remind your kids that after the break, they can come back to their video game. You're taking this break to give your brain a breather, not take away video games. It might also help kids to warn them that you'll do this. Tell them that they can play as much as they want to, but if they start to act tired or agitated, that it's time for a break. You're not villain-izing video games, or saying anything negative about their video games. You're simply trying to find balance in your life. It's a family goal, not a "fix my child" goal. The kids know the difference.

Incorporate video games into other activities. Kids really appreciate when we recognize their love for a video game outside of their gaming experience. Pokemon is a good example. There are books, movies, magazines, cards, http://www.pokemonlearningleague.com, and many other ways for us to support our kids' love of Pokemon when we are doing other things besides playing video games. Being enthusiastic about their video games gives them less reason to play video games in order to escape. It also encourages them to trust us, because we are showing them that we aren't taking a black and white approach against what they love to do.

Video Games May Hold the Key to Learning

There is something very compelling about video games. Kids will go through incredibly difficult challenges to meet the demands of a video game. They will learn how to read and do math in order to solve the problems the computer gives to them. Kids will also sit for hours and concentrate on the tasks in a game even when the tasks might be repetitive and boring.

These are all things that schools wish they could inspire kids to do. These are also often things that people successful in life are able to do. So what is it that video games provide that motivates kids to work so hard, for so long, without complaining?

I think we need to look at how video games are designed and implemented as a clue to how we can teach and motivate our own children. It's more important than ever that adults who teach children play these games, so they can understand the elements that draw kids in, and then can take those same elements and recreate them outside of the video game realm.

Video games are far from the enemy. In fact, they are the key to the future of education. Instead of trying to keep our kids away from video games, we need to encourage them to understand them, and use the skills they acquire in video games in other ventures. Most kids will do this without our help, because humans naturally take what is learned in one context and try to use that knowledge in another (hence, the need to deschool). But if we, as parents, understand and embrace the process of video games, we can help our children use the tools learned while playing games and make the connections when they are using them for other purposes.

In a lifestyle where we are learning in the world, everything runs together. The world is not divided into subjects. It's all interconnected. Computer games are one of the many things that bring us to a closer relationship to our world.

In an online interview at the World of Warcraft (WoW) Insider blog, one mom who plays this widely popular online video game said this about her family's experience playing games together: "[World of Warcraft] has led to many interesting conversations and research. For instance, one time my son and I played with a couple of guys from Brazil. One of the guys only typed in Portuguese; the other guy would translate. We got to learn a few Portuguese words, look up Brazil, and check time zones. We got to make a connection with stories from my husband about the time he was in Brazil (seeing shanty towns and eating the most tantalizing coconut pudding)."

This is not an unusual story. Video game playing is just one of the many ways we can connect with the world. When we don't make connections on a regular basis between the many things that we can do in the world, it's not that the connections aren't there; it's that we haven't backed up far enough to see them yet.

> **Laura's Story***: "Once I realized most of my concern about unlimited TV was about my own need for affirmation and acceptance as a good mom, I knew I needed to examine it. My kids really, really liked screen time. My husband grew up in a TV-watching family. (They had a collection of twenty videotapes and used a notebook to track their content. They'd cross off a show*

*after watching it, freeing up that particular cassette for re-
taping.) So three out of four family members desired more
screen time and I was elevating my dogma over their
desires. I really believed that if I loosened up my control,
they'd morph into zombies right in front of my eyes, never
to be rehabilitated. I really believed they'd never want to do
anything else. I really believed I'd be a bad mother. "It's
for your own good" type reasoning had taken up residence
in my brain. And while I railed against that sort of
authoritarianism in many realms, TV was different.*

I sure gave TV a lot of power.

*So we ate our organic food, used our earth-friendly cleaning
products, wore our resale clothes, and embraced our
dandelion-filled yard every spring. (Jonathan is still the
voice of reason on dandelions, proclaiming, each time I
cringe, "They're beautiful, mom. They're my favorite! A
whole yard of flowers!") And I pondered the idea of
loosening my control on screen time.*

*Turns out, there was no heralded announcement, "Now
you are FREE! Go forth and watch!" Rather, my control
began to quietly, gradually slip away. The kids would
watch or play beyond their time limit, and Rob and I
would argue about my unwillingness to be the screen-time
cop. They would beg to watch "just one more episode: or
play "just until I can get to a level where I can save" and I
would relent. They would forget they'd already used their
allotted time and sneak in more. It was exhausting. I felt
like the bad guy all the time, no matter what. If I
controlled their time, I felt like a warden. If I didn't, I felt
like a permissive parent. (Don't even get me started on
that derogatory slur often aimed at homeschoolers.) Rob
thought I was weak in my enforcement. The kids thought
I was unfair in my keeping-of-the-time. It was not fun.*

*And so gradually, ever-so-slowly, our rules about screen
time changed. Brady began showing an interest in
programming and designing, and I silently reasoned that*

those things were educational and as such, shouldn't be restricted. Rob and Jonathan began enjoying TV together more often, finding they both loved Sponge Bob and football. I found a few late-night TV shows I liked, revisiting my old college habit of indulging my night-owl tendencies.

It turns out, I'd given screen time more power than it had on its own. After the controls loosened, my kids did binge on screen time for a while, as we are all wont to do when we get our first taste of true freedom. But soon enough, they proved to me that nothing has that sort of control over a person, especially not a person who has a rich, varied life."

Above All, Relationships

Academic holes can always be filled in. Relationships with others and with ourselves, on the other hand, are much harder to mend. Keeping relationships of all kinds intact is more important than any academic knowledge, and is more important than doing homeschooling "right." Often times, what we think are homeschooling problems are actually emotional or relationship problems that extend through the whole family. Focusing on schoolwork or video games or other "problems" is often a distraction away from the real issues, which are commonly trust and connection problems between family members. We can see this is true, because so often, when relationships are strong, all of these superficial problems aren't much of an issue.

When we have strong relationships with our family members, problems are easier to deal with, and often don't even become problems – they are simply obstacles and opportunities.

Discover what makes you smile. And what makes your kids smile. Usually, we find that when we strengthen our relationships and increase trust, there is naturally a lot more to smile about.

Behavior that Makes Deschooling Difficult

A lot of attention is put on how our kids' attitudes towards learning and family make homeschooling difficult. We might think, "If only my child will (fill in the blank), homeschooling would be so much easier." The truth is that parents have just as much participation in the homeschool dance as children do. As you are going through your deschooling process, watch out for three common behaviors that parents often use, without even knowing it, which can make deschooling difficult for everyone.

Passive-aggressive behavior. This behavior is characterized by acting in a seemingly passive way in order to be aggressive. Giving someone the silent treatment is an example. Another would be making fun of someone with sarcasm. It can also appear in "fine, whatever" kind of responses, letting people make mistakes in order to be able to say, "I told you so," putting people into situations where they look like the bad guy, and blaming other people for problems. Ultimately, passive-aggressive behavior is a way to hide from one's own faults, and to make it look like we're the good guy, no matter what.

This kind of behavior destroys relationships. It makes people distrust us, it makes people stay very distanced from us, it keeps us from understanding others or being understood, and it keeps us from being able to deal with and get past real issues.

Bullying. This kind of behavior is any time we force other people to do what we want, or to admit we are better than them, in either explicit or implicit ways. It's when we use whatever power we have to bend people to our way of thinking or make them want to run away from us. This includes talking until the other person gives in, manipulation, not listening to the other person, getting other people to gang up on someone (i.e. parents ganging up on a kid, or getting other kids to help us convince the other to bend to our will), forcibly taking things away from people, threats, and physical violence.

Bully behavior pushes people from us, makes people not want to be around us, makes people afraid of us, and encourages rebellious behavior.

Right-fighting. This is probably one of the more subtle ways that we, as parents, can put a strain on our relationships. Some may have an issue with Dr. Phil McGraw and his approaches, but one of his catch phrases has a very true ring to it: "Do you want to be right, or do you want to be happy?"

It's easy to get on the "I'm right and I'll fight to prove it" train, and forget our true purpose. Our purpose is not to prove to our kids, our spouses, or the world, that we are right, but to support one another and make the world a better place.

Right-fighting ruins relationships because people will stop trying to communicate with us, our lives will be a series of battles rather than connections, and we make it clear that we don't care about what other people feel or think. Right-fighting is an ego-centric behavior, not one that encourages family cohesiveness.

All of these behaviors are normal human responses to the world around us. If we find ourselves exhibiting these behaviors from time to time, we're not doomed to homeschooling failure. However, it's important to admit to ourselves that we can be part of the problem, if there is one. Deschooling just won't work if we rely on unhealthy parental practices while we're trying to teach our children how to get along in the world without school.

Are We Doing Enough?

You might find that some days, everything is going great, and you feel like you've come a long way. Then, on other days, you might feel overcome with paranoia that you're not doing enough. This is a normal deschooling experience.

It's normal to vacillate between the school and no-school extremes. If you find yourself peacefully admiring the dust on top of the workbooks one day, and making a detailed schedule the next, be comforted that this is part of the process of finding your homeschooling balance.

My school instinct kicks in every time we step foot into a Barnes and Noble, or a homeschool conference. I love workbooks and lists. I can't resist the allure of multiple choice quizzes, rows of math exercises and in particular, grammar exercises! It's hard to pull myself out of a bookstore without getting at least one book for each kid.

I am excited about the idea of workbooks, and school, and planning and all that. But when we get home, and reality sets in, those workbooks aren't nearly as exciting. Especially when I realize that in order to get the kids to do them, I'd have to pretty much sit with them and hold their pencil for them. Workbooks always sound so great in theory, but reality doesn't always match the dream I have of how much the kids will love them.

So, then, I say "FINE!" to myself and swear I'll never bring out a workbook again. I'm going to be a bona fide 100% ultra-perfect unschooler! "Let's learn everything by digging in dirt and counting bugs!" Of course, that doesn't work either because I'm being reactionary with my hands in the air. Before long, the kids are prowling around the workbooks I have sworn off, spreading them all over the floor and, can you believe it, *doing them out of order*!

I'm in constant flux between micromanaging the kids' lives and letting things just happen on their own, when, in reality, the answer is somewhere in the middle. It's extremely hard to stay in the middle though. And where in the middle should I be?

If you find yourself going in and out of the middle, exploring the far reaches of the educational suburbs, don't beat yourself up over it. Bring out those family and educational goals, get out of the house, and distract yourself a little from those nagging should monsters, until you remember where the middle is for your family. Staying there as long as you can until another bout of schizophrenia hits, and then repeat. Be ready to repeat it a lot. And smile, you're going through the normal roller coaster of learning to live without school.

Diane Flynn Keith talks about vacillating between the two extremes, and that it's normal and OK. In her article, *A Recovery Program for Homeschool Split Personality Disorder*, Diane says "Do you vacillate between child-led, developmentally appropriate, interest-initiated unschooling on one hand, and traditional, structured, academic-based education on the other? These mood-altering swings in methodology creep up unexpectedly on homeschooling parents and are often exacerbated by events beyond their control. I know. I am recovering from homeschool split-personality disorder."

Dealing with Criticism

You may also find the paranoia coming from other people, in the form of criticism. It's particularly hard to hear from family and friends. Here are some ideas on how to deal with the paranoia brought on by "concerned" friends and family on homeschooling.

- Do your best to surround yourself with people who will support you and your decision to homeschool..
- Remember, criticism tells us more about them, than it does about us.
- Listen to and acknowledge people who want to undermine your attempt to have your own independent mind, then let them go.
- Let experience and time be the proof that what you're doing is OK.
- Bring the focus back into the family, focusing on keeping relationships strong before worrying about being judged or being wrong.
- Take it seriously to address the grievances inside the immediate family (parents and kids), while letting go of the pressure outside of the family unit.
- Listening and distraction: "That's a really interesting point. It reminds me of a story I read in the paper about the teacher who won the Nobel Prize."
- Being prepared with a standard response for the "big" questions: "We're not sure how long we'll homeschool. Right now it works. We're taking it a day at a time."
- Redirecting the topic back to the speaker: People love to talk about themselves. "What do you think of the problem of kids in school graduating but not being able to read?"

- Smiling and nodding: "I see what you're saying." Just because we understand doesn't mean we have to agree, or that we have to argue when we don't agree.

As with family members, relationships always come first. Ideals are important, but they aren't as important as relationships. Even with people who are our friends, there will be times we don't agree on important issues. Homeschooling is just like any other issue. Taking offense to others not understanding homeschooling is a choice we make. We have to think hard about what's more important, our relationship with our friend, or our need to convince them we made a good choice.

> **Shari's Story**: *"You know, when I first started homeschooling I was much more concerned about what people had to say or thought about it. I have now learned that there are a few people that are genuinely interested in what we are doing and how it works. The rest have an axe to grind or need to be right and those are the folks we collectively just shine on! We answer their questions in a way we know will make them most comfortable and pretty much just don't engage in any debates or polarizing type of discussions. It really works too!! All those long time homeschoolers that kept advising I not worry about it and just not engage in discussions were absolutely right.*
>
> *As far as family members finding fault because of homeschooling, I can pretty much guarantee these same folks find fault with what children are being fed, how their parents spend their money, where they go on vacation and so on. Let's face it, there will always be a vegan sister in law horrified by meat eaters, an ultra conservative aunt preaching the dangers of the latest kid's movie or a clean freak cousin disgusted that the family dog is allowed on the sofa. In other words, busy bodies are going to put their nose in other people's business, whether they homeschool or not!"*

Self-Discovery Questions

- What is the one thing you'd like to change? How can you implement a change in the family that will create what everyone in the family would consider a positive move forward?

- What is your natural rhythm? If you had nothing telling you what to do, when to do, or where to go, what would your family's rhythm be? How can you arrange your life so that you're working as much as you can within that rhythm?

- Do you feel like you are scattered and worrying about many things at once? Which one worry is the most stress-causing? Is there an underlying issue that causing this stress? Is there something fundamental that can be changed which would ease stress, such as increasing family closeness, understanding or communication?

- Do you know a family that just seems to be in sync with each other? How do they handle stress? How do they handle conflict? Is that family being true to themselves?

- Imagine for a moment that school did not exist. How many stressors in your life would be instantly better?

- What is good in your life without school? How can you create more of that kind of good in your deschooling life?

Step 10: Step Away from "Deschooling"

"When you're finished changing, you're finished."
- *Benjamin Franklin*

"One of the greatest discoveries a man makes, one of his greatest surprises, is to find he can do what he was afraid he couldn't."
- *Henry Ford*

Signs That Deschooling Is Over

In my opinion, most of us never really stop deschooling. Just as, when we move to a new country and culture, we never really lose the influence of our original cultural upbringing, even if we completely integrate into our new environment.

Deschooling is the process of discovering who we are within the bigger context of our society. Who we are always changes. There is always more to learn about ourselves. Plus, the pressure of judging ourselves by external factors will always there. It's a life-long balance of being authentic and living in our modern society. Becoming successful is a never-ending process of discovering who we are and the world around us. We can never truly leave the culture that we are a part of. School is an integral part of who we are as a society; so much so, that to completely deschool would be to remove ourselves from the world we live in. Realistically, we will be deschooling the rest of our lives.

However, there's a point where we are no longer *primarily* deschooling, where we are now homeschooling and living, with a little bit of deschooling in the background as a kind of life-management.

Before we get to the point where we generally feel comfortable in our homeschooling skin, it's normal to go back and forth between being in control, and feeling like no matter what we do, the world doesn't seem to want to cooperate. We find ourselves repeating the deschooling process over and over, in order to keep rediscovering who we are, both as an individual and as a family. The downside of this process is that it takes work. The upside is the knowledge that we are never done growing. There is always movement forward.

And of course, as the children grow and change, new challenges will appear, turning everything upside down on its head. When this happens, it's natural to want to cling to our old ways. Grabbing hold of what we know is the mind's way of dealing with stress. When we do that, it's time to deschool ourselves, yet again, and figure out which of our decisions are being made because of what's in front of us, or being made because of what we think our 3rd grade teacher would say.

But, there is a pretty good way to know when the initial, harrowing, life-changing, mind-changing deschooling process is over, and we've arrived at a certain state of maintenance.

12 Signs You're Done Deschooling

The kids wake up every morning generally happy and looking forward to what the day brings. (Exception: when you have a night owl. Then, they don't want to go to sleep because there's so much to DO! They don't want to put if off until tomorrow.)

When you look at a curriculum, or class, or book, or field trip, you have a pretty good idea if your kids will enjoy it or not. (And, if they don't end up liking it when you thought they would, it's not a big deal. You use it as information for the future.)

You see yourself as a learner too.

You often have "Wow, my kids are so interesting!" moments.

You know what your family philosophy is, and what "learning" and "success" mean to you, independent of what it means in the world around you.

Your kids aren't afraid to bring up the topic of school. In fact, they are willing to go to you about pretty much everything, even if it's controversial, embarrassing, or illegal. They trust you, and you trust them. (Doesn't mean things are perfect, but the lines of communication are open.)

You love being around your kids. (Although, we all do need a little bit of a break sometimes, even from the people we love to be around. So, you also make sure to find time for yourself when you need it.)

When you think about learning, you're excited and enthusiastic.

You realize that "doing a good job" has little to do with how many boxes you check off your to-do list. It also has little to do with how many worksheets you get done, or how well the kids do on a test, but by the internal gauge that only your family, and the members of your family, can understand.

You feel like you belong in the world. There's no end in sight to all the amazing things there are to discover out there.

Education and life mesh with everyone's personalities, interests, and abilities. Nobody is clamoring for a break, such as summer or a vacation.

Lastly, and perhaps most importantly, you trust your children, you trust yourself, and when change challenges you, that trust keeps everyone strong.

Saying Goodbye to Fear

The magic formula to move into a fearless life is to live in a way that reflects who we are. We can make decisions to be proud of – not because they are the "right" decisions, but because they are decisions that clearly take into account the things that are important to us as individuals, and to our family as a unit. If the grounding of our decisions continues to be based on our goals, life-long deschooling and learning won't get derailed too long before we regain our footing in the path of becoming a better "us".

So when we look back, and perhaps see where we made mistakes, we can honestly say, "I did the best I could with what I had, and I wouldn't change a thing. We had a great time on the journey. Right now, I see I made a mistake, and we're dealing with the results of that now. But it will get better, because I know who I am, who my kids are, and I'm willing to let go of the voices that tell me what I'm "supposed" to be doing, and do instead, what works for us."

We've made it to the other side when we look back at the history of our kids' educations at home and we see all the things we did right. If we can find insight where our kids failed, and inspiration where they grew and became better people, we can say deschooling is over. School teaches us to focus on our problems and then try to fix them. Deschooled kids and parents focus on where we are strong, and how we can take advantage of those strengths. Our weaknesses are only important if they keep us from our goals. In which case, they are obstacles to be overcome, not problems to be fixed.

Children are part of human existence. Having weaknesses is not a weakness. Seeing weaknesses as problems and trying to make them go away, is. We can never make weaknesses fully go away. We can accept them and use the energy towards growing rather than trying to make up for faults.

For ourselves as parents, we have to look at what our strengths are, and use those strengths to teach our kids. If we focus on what we can't do well (say, organizing or motivating the kids to do school work), we are trapped in the same school cycle of ignoring our strengths to fix our problems, and we end up not being all that great at anything. If we focus on what we do well as homeschool parents, and use that as our primary tool for educating our kids, we'll be far more successful, happy and true to ourselves than if we try to teach them in a way that doesn't match up to who we are.

We are deschooled when we can see that we are all capable, strong people, in one way or another, and that we are all weak, incapable, and problematic people in other ways. And even though we know that, we spend most of our time on what makes us stronger, more capable and happier – and only spend the absolute minimum possible on the things that make it clear to ourselves how incapable we are.

Nobody has the perfect formula for your success, except you. If you don't feel like you're done deschooling, keep moving forward. Keep the search for yourself and your family going. Enjoy the world around you until you've settled into your new life. Then, keep enjoying the world like a bowl of ice cream.

You may get to the point where you don't even realize that you're deschooling anymore. And perhaps, that's the point where it's actually over, when we're no longer worried if we're done or not, and we're just living and learning together one interesting moment at a time.

Reducing Stress While Deschooling

Deschooling can be a roller coaster ride of twists, turns and sudden drops. It can be thrilling and it can be frightening. During your journey, if you find yourself overcome with stress, try these tips to bring you back to your center.

Creative visualization. Take yourself away from your current moment and think about what your perfect day would look like. Start with waking up in the morning and do a mental walk-through of every aspect of your day, unfolding in a way that makes you feel good. After you are done, open your eyes, and carry this image around with you. This image is not of what you expect or want to happen, but an image of what can happen. It might not happen this very second, but it can. Keep your awareness open to this possibility.

Meditation, prayer, or breathing. Having quiet moments to ourselves where we focus on our breathing and calm our thoughts is a timeless approach to stress reduction. Not only does the practice of meditation, prayer, or just breathing give us a moment to recover our center, it also gives us practice for dealing with stress later. The more we take time to breathe when we are calm, the easier it is to breathe and relax when we are dealing with stressful situations later. It's not a quick fix, but a general practice for having a more centered and calm approach to life.

Remove ourselves. Simply removing ourselves from a situation can help diffuse it. Sometimes, we have no idea of how much our own behavior is creating the stress around us. If we take a moment to step back from a stressful situation, we might find that it takes care of itself, or we might be able to see better choices that will help the situation, or at least not make it worse. In Buddhism, there's a saying, "First, do no harm." This means that in any situation, being helpful is important, but if we can't be helpful, at least do not harm others by our actions.

Yoga, tai chi, walking. All three of these activities are wonderful for calming the mind, and getting through our mental baggage. Our minds are distinctly connected to our bodies. When we move our bodies in a positive, calm way, it encourages us to bring our minds to that place as well. Also, yoga, tai chi and walking all encourage breathing, which increases blood flow to the brain. Often, when we are stressed, we breathe in short, low-oxygen strokes. This reduces oxygen to the brain, which makes it harder to think clearly. Moving slowly and breathing deeply brings us to our center and helps us make better choices.

Minimize and simplify. Often times, we are stressed because we are trying to squeeze too much into one day, do too many things at once, or trying to fix too many problems. By simplifying our lives, we can reduce stress. We also can be more effect problem solvers. In addition, living simply is more satisfying, because we have time and space to appreciate what we have.

Delegate tasks and responsibility. Another way to deal with having too much to do, or feeling like we have to do everything, is to delegate tasks. But not only should we delegate the task, but delegate the ownership of that task. There is nothing more stressful than giving someone a task and still holding on to the responsibility of getting that task done. Not only do we want the thing done, but then we also have to deal with making sure the other person done it! If we give other people tasks to do without giving up the ownership of whether that thing is done or not, we are creating more work for ourselves, not less.

Smile on purpose. It's a lot of work to be upset. It's actually a lot easier to be happy and satisfied. Being happy is choice. If things aren't going the way we want, or we are stressed, we can make the choice to smile on purpose. By physically smiling, we have taken the first step towards making the conscious choice to be happy. It's one of the many ways to help us look past our frustration and through to a solution.

Look for what is right, and for the good. Humans spend so much time stressing over what's not working or what is wrong with the world. The answer to making things better and being happier is to spend more time looking at what's right, and how the things we are going through have some good in them. Reduce stress by making a choice to acknowledge when things are right. Not only will you be happier, the people around you will be too.

Final Words

My goal for this book was to talk about how anyone can ease through the deschooling process. After reading *Deschooling Gently*, I hope that you have moved, at least a little bit, from "how do we do this?" to "we're on the right track!"

So this is where I depart and you take over. You have everything you need to succeed in you. You can do it, and you will. I trust you.

I hope that I have written myself out of a job and that you'll put down this book, look up and smile, and continue on with your homeschooling life with strength and fearlessness.

Happy Homeschooling!

Self-Discovery Questions:

- Do you feel comfortable in your new life? Is everyone generally happy and excited to be alive?
- Does the idea of school make you nervous? If so, why does school still have a hold on you?
- Do you feel confident that the last word ends with you? That it's important to acknowledge the world around us, but ultimately, it's only you who has the ultimate authority in deciding what is considered a "good" education?
- Are you confident that no matter what happens, your kids are going to succeed and live a good life? You should be. Because it's true.

Appendix A

Resources for Homeschoolers and Life Learners

Online

Laws and Legalities

About.com Legal Resources:
http://homeschooling.about.com/od/legal/Staying_Legal_Homeschool_Laws_and_Requirements.htm

Or

http://homeschooling.about.com/cs/gettingstarted/a/legalusa.htm

A2Z Home'sCool Legal Resources:
http://homeschooling.gomilpitas.com/directory/Legalities.htm

Homeschool Legal Defense Association:
http://www.hslda.org/laws/default.asp

Homeschooling Support

About.com Support Groups by State:
http://homeschooling.about.com/od/casg/Support_Groups_California.htm

A2Z Home'sCool Discussion List. An eclectic group of home-schoolers who discuss anything and everything that has to do with homeschooling.
http://groups.yahoo.com/group/A2Zhomescool

A2Z Home'sCool Homeschool Support Group Listings by Region:
http://homeschooling.gomilpitas.com/weblinks/support.htm

Best Homeschooling. Many articles about homeschooling and education as a family.
http://www.besthomeschooling.org

Excellence in Education Game Curriculum:
http://www.excellenceineducation.com
(626) 821-0025

Homefires Homeschooled Teen Resources:
http://www.homefires.com

HomefiresJournal Discussion List. Another inclusive group with lots of ideas and support. This group offers a monthly curriculum exchange as well as open political and practical discussion of alternative approaches to education.
http://groups.yahoo.com/group/HomefiresJournal

HomeschoolingCreatively Discussion List. Although this group's purpose is to create a community for parents with children who are "right-brained" learners, the discussions are often useful to any kind of learner. The list is also inclusive and welcoming.
http://groups.yahoo.com/group/homeschoolingcreatively

Universal Preschool. Website all about homeschooling children ages birth through 5.
http://www.universalpreschool.com

Yahoo e-Mailing Lists:
http://groups.yahoo.com keyword search "homeschool" "(your area)"

Deschooling Resources:

John Taylor Gatto's website on learning without school:
http://www.johntaylorgatto.com

LifeWithoutSchool Blog:
http://lifewithoutschool.typepad.com

Links to various articles and perspectives on deschooling:
http://homeschooling.gomilpitas.com/weblinks/deschooling.htm

Sandra Dodd's Essay and Links on deschooling:
http://sandradodd.com/deschooling

Donahue-Krueger, Pattie. "Deschooling," 1998.
http://sandradodd.com/pattiedeschooling

Warshaw, Meredith G. "Deschooling on the Road," *Home Educator's Family Times*, July/August 2003, Volume 11, Issue 4.
http://www.homeeducator.com/FamilyTimes/articles/11-4article12.htm

Tammy Takahashi's Deschooling and Alternative Education Blog:
http://justenough.wordpress.com

Other Online Educational Resources

Benetta, William J. "How a Public School in Scottsdale, Arizona, Subjected Students to Islamic Indoctrination," *Textbook League*. An article on the process of how textbooks are influenced by special interest groups.
http://www.textbookleague.org/tci-az.htm

Carmichael, Mary. "Can Exercise Make You Smarter?" *Newsweek*, Mar 26, 2007.
http://www.newsweek.com/id/36056

Clark, Donald. "A Time Capsule of Training and Learning," 2008. An overview of the history training and learning through the ages, starting with 5th century B.C. China to modern day computer-based and consumer-based training.
http://www.skagitwatershed.org/~donclark/hrd/history/history2.html

Feynman, Richard P. "Judging Books by Their Covers," *Text Book Letter*, July/August 1999. Feynman's experiences with public school math textbook selection, and commentary from other teachers and administrators about textbook selection.
http://www.textbookleague.org/103feyn.htm

Forte, Carolyn. "A Game Plan for Learning," *The Link Homeschool News Network*, Volume 6, Issue 2.
http://www.homeschoolnewslink.com/homeschool/articles/vol6iss2/learningwithgames.shtml

Meier, Deborah. "Educating a Democracy: Standards and the future of public education," *Boston Review*, 2000. Essay on why the standards are ruining our schools (and several rebuttals to her original article).
http://bostonreview.net/BR24.6/meier.html

MIT Open Courseware. Hundreds of MIT courses available for free online.
http://ocw.mit.edu

Poisso, Lisa. 15 Minutes of Fame: Horde of Unschoolers," *WoW Insider Blog*, January 15, 2008. An interview with "Takulah", a member of an unschooling guild in the World of Warcraft.
http://www.wowinsider.com/2008/01/15/15-minutes-of-fame-horde-of-unschoolers

Ray, Brian D. "Homeschoolers on to College: What the Research Shows Us," *Journal of College Admission*, Fall 2004. A synopsis of ten years of research and studies about homeschooling.
http://findarticles.com/p/articles/mi_qa3955/is_200410/ai_n9443747/pg_1

Sheppard, Keith and Dennis M. Robbins. "High School Biology Today: What the Committee of Ten Actually Said," *CBE-Life Sciences Education*, May 21, 2007.
http://www.lifescied.org/cgi/content/full/6/3/198

Stille, Alexander. "Textbook Publishers Learn: Avoid Messing With Texas," *New York Times*, June 29, 2002. Article about the public school textbook controversy.
http://query.nytimes.com/gst/fullpage.html?res=9F0CE7DC113EF93AA15755C0A9649C8B63

Books

Armstrong, Thomas. *In Their Own Way – Discovering and Encouraging Your Child's Multiple Intelligences.* Tarcher, 2000. Although written primarily for parents with children in school, it examines the way that we expect children to learn, and gives clear advice on how to help our children learn according to their unique needs.

Ben-Shahar, Tal. Happier: *Learn the Secrets to Daily Joy and Lasting Fulfillment.* McGraw-Hill, 2007. This is one of my favorite non-self-help books on life fulfillment. Based on research, Ben-Shahar reflects on the true nature of what happiness is in our culture, and how we can attain it. Many of his examples show how school actually discourages us from finding true happiness.

Buscaglia, Leo F. *Personhood: The Art of Being Fully Human.* Ballantine Books, 1986. When I first read this book, I was shocked by how much it paralleled our homeschooling purpose. This is not a homeschooling book. This is a book about what it means to be a successful human being.

Dobson, Linda. *The Art of Education: Reclaiming Your Family, Community, and Self.* Holt Associates, 1997. Although out of print, I had to list this book, because it encompasses everything deschooling is about. Anything by Dobson is worth reading. If you can get a hold of this one early on in your homeschooling journey, grab it up!

Dobson, Linda. *Ultimate Book of Homeschooling Ideas.* Three Rivers Press, 2002. This is one of my favorite books to recommend to new homeschoolers. It's a good reference manual for those days when you feel like you aren't doing enough, or that you want more variety. This should be a staple for all homeschooling households.

Faber, Adele and Elain Mazlish. *How to Talk So Your kids Will Listen, How to Listen So Your Kids Will Talk*. Collins, 1999. For some, this book might be elementary. For me, reading this book was a light bulb moment in learning how to communicate with my children.

Greene, Rebecca. *The Teenager's Guide to School Outside the Box*. Free Spirit Publishing, 2000. This is the deschooling guide for teens, in disguise. If you have a teen who is deschooling, this is a must-read.

Guterson, David. *Family Matters: Why Homeschooling Makes Sense*. Harvest Books, 193. This book has a bit of nostalgia for me. It was the book that convinced me homeschooling was going to work for us. I liked this book because it's written by a high school English teacher whose wife homeschools their sons. Being in both worlds gives Guterson a unique perspective.

Hern, Matt. *Deschooling Our Lives*. New Society Publishers, 1996. Although this book is currently out of print, it is a deschooling classic. If you can find a copy, snag it up!

Holt, John. *How Children Fail*. Perseus Publishing, 1995. This is an important book because it outlines many of the pitfalls of education, and why children, who are born natural learners, often end up uninterested in school.

Holt, John. *Learning All the Time*. Addison Wesley Publishing Company, 1990. Anything by John Holt is a winner. He has been called the father of the modern homeschooling movement, due to his criticism of today's school practices. *Learning All the Time* is his last, and arguably his best, book. It sums up his perspectives on education, focussing mainly on early education.

Illich, Ivan. *Deschooling Society*. Marion Boyars Publishers, 1996. This is the book that introduced the concept of "deschooling". The 1996 edition is the most recent version. The original was published in 1972.

Kohn, Alfie. *The Homework Myth*. Da Capo Lifelong Books, 2007. This updated version of Kohn's groundbreaking work shows us why homework isn't the path to real learning. Although not intended for homeschoolers necessarily, *The Homework Myth* brings up important points of why giving our kids even more work isn't going to make them smarter.

Kohn, Alfie. *Punished by Rewards*. Replica Books, 2001. Rewards are a huge part of how schools motivate children to do the work they are supposed to do. Unfortunately, rewards have significant drawbacks. If you are thinking of using stickers, stars, and money to get your kids to do their work, read this book first.

Kohn, Alfie. *Unconditional Parenting*. Atria, 2006. Since deschooling is so much about parenting, I often recommend this book to new homeschoolers.

Lahrson-Fisher, Ann. *Fundamentals of Homeschooling: Notes on Successful Family Living*. Nettlepatch Press, 2002. This is a gem that does not get enough attention. It includes information on practically everything having to do with homeschooling. It's a great book for new homeschoolers.

Llewellyn, Grace. *Real Lives: Eleven Teenagers Who Don't Go to School Tell Their Own Stories*. Lowry House Publishers, 2005. Eleven stories of children who grew up without school. Make sure to get the 2nd edition, which has "during" and "after" stories of all the teens.

Llewellyn, Grace. *The Teenage Liberation Handbook: How to Quit School and Get a Real Life and Education*. Lowry House Pub, 1998. If it weren't for this book, you wouldn't be reading *Deschooling Gently*. *The Teenage Liberation Handbook* was the first book I read about homeschooling. I remember reading it as an adult, and thinking how I wanted to drop-ship boxes of this book to our local high schools.

Willis, Mariaemma and Victoria Kindle Hodson. *Discover Your Child's Learning Style: Children Learn in Unique Ways*. Prima Lifestyles, 1999. A complete guide on learning styles, with an in-depth test to understand a person's learning preferences.

Magazines and Newspapers

Home Education Magazine
http://www.homeedmag.com

Life Learning Magazine
http://www.lifelearningmagazine.com

The Link Homeschooling Newspaper
http://www.homeschoolnewslink.com

Live Free Learn Free
http://www.livefreelearnfree.com

Old Schoolhouse Magazine
http://www.thehomeschoolmagazine.com

Secular Homeschooler
http://www.secular-homeschooling.com

FAQ: Frequently Asked Questions About Deschooling

Q. What is deschooling?

A. Deschooling is the process of getting used to learning as a family without the external control of a school system. Some call it a decompression time, or a vacation. Generally, it involves doing less schoolwork and more life work, less judging and more exploring, less have-tos and more want-tos. Deschooling is moving toward a life where everyone is happy and learning.

Deschooling unfolds differently for every family. The 'how's and 'what's of your family will probably be unique. The 'why' of deschooling we all share: to find out who we are and what the best learning path is for our children.

Q. Why and when do we need to deschool?

A. When we leave the modern school model to create a family-oriented educational environment, it's not clear what the first steps should be. We don't want to do things the way we used to, because it wasn't working. Yet turning away from the biggest educational system in our culture, we see before us a blur of methods, gurus, curriculum, philosophies, and advice. Where do we even start to weed through all of that and pick the right path for our family?

Deschooling is learning how to live without being in school, to fend for ourselves, and to provide our children with an appropriate educational environment. For some, this process only is necessary right after leaving school, for they find their footing quickly. For others, this process is a long-term endeavor, constantly making adjustments to recover and maintain the love of learning we were all born with.

For those us who have never sent our child to school, most of us still may need to deschool ourselves from the educational world we grew up in. Our old knowledge of how to learn and teach is still ingrained in our personal histories. When we've decided to take responsibility to teach our children, we need tools to help them learn. Deschooling ourselves is how we find the tools we need, even if our kids never have been to school.

Living and learning at home in a world where everyone has been raised with school process being the only way, most of us need some level of deschooling. Even if it's just enough to say with confidence, "We are satisfied with the choices we've made." *Deschooling Gently* is a step by step guide to helping you gain that confidence.

Q. What happens if we don't deschool?

A. Families who hang on to the old ways of schooling while educating at home have a choice – either they have to create an atmosphere where the parent is the ultimate authority and the child must obey or suffer school-type consequences, or they must find an exterior source to keep their children motivated to do school work. If we don't deschool, our children are caught in the same external reward loop that exists in school.

It becomes challenging, although not impossible for sure, to keep a child's love of learning alive when the biggest motivation to learn is from the outside. Deschooling teaches us how to find our internal motivation, and learn to trust ourselves and each other. If we don't deschool, it doesn't guarantee homeschooling failure, but it does make it more difficult to find educational freedom.

Q. Who is deschooling for, the kids or parents?

A. In a nutshell, both. Even if there is only one family member who is having a particularly difficult time with the transition from school to home learning, deschooling is a family process. The one member who is "acting up" is merely a symptom of the entire dynamic of the family. If one person needs to deschool, everyone does.

Q. Will deschooling change our lives?

A. Absolutely. Deschooling will forever change the way you look at education. Even if you only homeschool for a short time, having deschooled will change the way you look at education and what it's for.

Deschooling will also affect your children's relationship with learning. They understand, either explicitly or intrinsically, that true learning comes from their own soul, not the needs of others to see them perform.

Q. How long will it take?

A. That's hard to say. For some, they feel deschooled after a few months. For other families, it continues for a lifetime. I have to admit, however, that after a while, I started to see how much positive change that deschooling has brought to my life, and now I look forward to more. Deschooling might feel like a struggle in the beginning, because we are trying to replace old habits of thinking about education. It takes time to change long-ago established patterns. *Deschooling Gently* is designed to offer you an approach that minimizes possible grief in the beginning of the deschooling process.

Q. What if my wife/husband/significant other isn't on board with the deschooling?

A. A lot of what deschooling is about involves being close as a family, understanding one another and communicating. These things can be done without bringing up the word "deschool". If your spouse or significant other is intimidated by what might seem like a formal process, or a big change, you can still make great strides in affecting the way your family works together by working on your own perspectives on education.

Most deschooling ideas are simple and don't involve have-to's or forced events. That way, you can work with everyone's interests and strengths whether or not they are interested in deschooling.

Q. Do most people deschool?

A. To a certain extent, almost every homeschooling family goes through a deschooling process of one kind or another. Some decide explicitly to take time off to deschool, while others prefer to let hit happen organically as they learn their own style. Any family that makes decisions on how to educate based on their own beliefs and perspectives has gone through some form of deschooling process.

On the other hand, not all families deschool completely. And by "completely", I mean that the family makes all of their educational decisions without the aid of an outside influence such as a teacher, program or curriculum.

I must emphasize that deschooling completely is not the goal I advocate. I advocate finding your educational happiness, wherever that lands you. The process of deschooling gives you permission to do that. It does not require you to teach a certain way, or choose a specific educational approach.

Q. Does deschooling mean you're not teaching?

A. Yes and no. Deschooling is a different way of looking at teaching and learning. Deschooled learning outside of a school setting is heavily based on a family's needs and not on an expert's idea of how, what and when children should be taught. Although some families choose to use traditional teacher-to-student teaching methods during deschooling, we aren't limited to that approach. We are free to use whatever kind of educational methods we'd like, including, but not limited to, mentoring, setting an example, giving responsibility, natural consequences, making suggestions, family projects, and outside classes.

There is a lot of learning and educating going on during deschooling. And depending on what your definition of teaching is, there is a lot of that too. But it looks different from school in most cases. That's OK because the whole point of deschooling is that it doesn't matter what it looks like on the outside, so long as everyone's needs are met.

Q. Will the kids get behind if we deschool?

A. I'm going to be honest here and say that yes, there is a possibility that a child will get behind the school's schedule if a family spends significant time deschooling. On the other hand, there is a possibility that a child will speed very far ahead as well.

Schools have a pace and scope that precisely marks what and when a group of children will learn something. When we remove ourselves from that track, and learn things according to any other pace and scope, we'll lose our lockstep with the local school process. Some things we'll miss while the school is covering that material, other things we'll learn while the school kids are missing out.

If providing an education parallel to your local school pace and scope is your desire, deschooling may not be for you. You can't be free and be entrenched at the same time. You can't go by someone else's pace and at your own pace at the same time. You have to make a choice.

Q. Will my child be able to go back to school one day if we deschool?

A. Yes. Most homeschooled children, even those who spend years learning at their own pace, eventually enter into some form of formal learning environment. And just like their schooled counterparts, they adjust to the demands of the program. Depending on the child's temperament, age, past experience and learning style, how quickly they adjust will vary.

There are a few exceptions to this, including reentry into high school grades 10, 11 or 12. Many high schools resist placing a student by age when they haven't had traditional school courses. If your teen is interested in entering high school after the 9th grade, call the school early to find out their requirements for non-traditional students.

Q. Can a deschooled teen get into college?

A. Yes. Deschooled teens apply to college much in the same way as adults who have been out of school for a while do. That is to say, they don't typically use the traditional front door method that everyone else is using.

The good news is that kids who don't have a traditional transcript will often have credit from community college, real life experience, and a clear idea of what they want to accomplish in college. These students often apply as 2nd semester freshmen or sophomores. There have even been teens who took so many core classes at the community college level, that they entered college as a junior. Since they are not competing with the thousands of other 18-year-old freshmen, their chances of being accepted are slightly higher.

The bad news is that a teen that hasn't gone through the traditional system will have to do a lot more research and paperwork to find out how to apply to an institution of higher education. Each college has their own way of processing non-traditional student applications. Also, some state and other publicly funded colleges have stringent application requirements that put non-traditional students at a disadvantage.

If college is important to your teen, make sure to do your research early. Talking to other homeschoolers in the local area who have gone through the process, reading books like *The Teenage Liberation Handbook* by Grace Llewellyn and *The Teenager's Guide to School Outside the Box* by Rebecca Greene and talking directly to admissions officers at the schools your teen is interested in will make the transition smoother.

Q. Where did the idea of "deschooling" come from?

A. The term "deschooling" was coined by Austrian-born philosopher Ivan Illich in his 1971 book *Deschooling Society*. Since then, it has been used in the homeschooling community with various meanings. Matt Hern wrote a book entitled *Deschooling Our Lives* in 1996 that revisited Illich's perspective that real education and learning is incompatible with today's school system.

Today, "deschooling" is used in many homeschooling circles to describe the detox time after leaving school and moving to a more relaxed approach to education. The undercurrent of the term still resides, implying that this break from school is to give us space to discover how to learn without limits or constraints—an idea that is closer to Ivan Illich's original idea of real learning.

In his forward for *Deschooling Our Lives*, Ivan Illich writes, "If the means for learning (in general) are abundant, rather than scarce, then education never arises – one does not need to make special arrangements for "learning." If, on the other hand, the means for learning are in scarce supply, or are assumed to be scarce, then educational arrangements crop up to "ensure" that certain important knowledge, ideas, skills, attitudes, etc., are "transmitted." Education then becomes an economic commodity which one consumes, or, to use common language, which one "gets."

The roots of term "deschooling" roots still remain, in that it is often used to convey the idea that access to learning and knowledge is abundant, and it's readily available out of the confines of school walls.

Q. Does deschooling mean you're anti-education or anti-school?

A. Not necessarily. It's true that politically, the two ideas often go hand in hand. However, deschooling is ultimately a personal journey. How you see education, learning, and knowledge is up to you. You may find that through deschooling, formal education will become less appealing, but that doesn't mean that you'll necessarily grow to be against it politically. Many families who have deschooled aren't against education, but it's not uncommon that they question its current applications and purpose in our schools.

Q. Does deschooling mean we just leave the kids alone and let them do whatever they want?

A. Absolutely not. In fact, deschooling is about coming together more than ever before. It gives us a chance to know each other, spend time together and enjoy life together. There will be periods that we separate to do our own projects – maybe even long stretches of time. But overall, the total amount of time spent together as a family is increased compared to a school life.

Deschooling doesn't mean we let our children do whatever they want to. They can do more of what they want to and less of what they don't. But everyone is still a family, and as such, everyone has to work together, sometimes doing things they don't want in order to keep harmony. However, the goal is to reduce the amount that this happens so that everyone feels like they are getting their needs met. This requires a lot of being together, communicating and negotiating. Just like real life.

Q. Does deschooling mean letting my child play video games all day?

A. Not necessarily. Video games seem to be the biggest worry among deschooling parents. Of all the activities that kids can do when they are deschooling, video games seems to be top pick.

If you are worried that playing a lot of video games during deschooling is detrimental to your family's relationships, there are ways to encourage kids to do other things besides video games that don't involve coercing, arguing, or arbitrary time limits. *Deschooling Gently* explores ways to connect as a family, and learn, while still having time to relax and enjoy our hobbies.

Printed in the United States
208601BV00003BA/102/P